*Reframing*
# EVALUATION
*Through*
APPRECIATIVE
QUIRY

| AP 10 07 | DATE DUE | | |
|---|---|---|---|
| | | | |
| | | | |
| | | | |
| | | | |
| | | | |
| | | | |
| | | | |
| | | | |
| | | | |
| | | | |

# *Reframing* EVALUATION *Through* APPRECIATIVE INQUIRY

## Hallie Preskill
*Claremont Graduate University*

## Tessie Tzavaras Catsambas
*EnCompass LLC*

SAGE Publications
Thousand Oaks ▪ London ▪ New Delhi

*For information:*

Sage Publications, Inc.
2455 Teller Road
Thousand Oaks, California 91320
E-mail: order@sagepub.com

Sage Publications Ltd.
1 Oliver's Yard
55 City Road
London EC1Y 1SP
United Kingdom

Sage Publications India Pvt. Ltd.
B-42, Panchsheel Enclave
Post Box 4109
New Delhi 110 017  India

Printed in the United States of America

*Library of Congress Cataloging-in-Publication Data*

Preskill, Hallie S.
Reframing evaluation through appreciative inquiry / Hallie Preskill,
Tessie Tzavaras Catsambas.
     p. cm.
Includes bibliographical references and index.
ISBN 1-4129-0951-1 (pbk.)
    1. Organizational change. 2. Organizational effectiveness. 3. Evaluation.
I. Catsambas, Tessie Tzavaras. II. Title.
HD58.8.P736 2006
658.4′013—dc22                                        2006004827

This book is printed on acid-free paper.

06   07   08   09   10   10   9   8   7   6   5   4   3   2   1

| | |
|---|---|
| *Acquisitions Editor:* | Lisa Cuevas Shaw |
| *Associate Editor:* | Margo Beth Crouppen |
| *Editorial Assistant:* | Karen Greene |
| *Production Editor:* | Laureen A. Shea |
| *Typesetter:* | C&M Digitals (P) Ltd. |
| *Cover Designer:* | Janet Foulger |

# Contents

# Table of Case Examples

| Chapter | Case Number | Case Example |
|---|---|---|
| Chapter 1: Introducing Appreciative Inquiry | 1 | Developing successful collaborations at the Centers for Disease Control and Prevention (CDC) |
| | 2 | Using Appreciative Inquiry at Evergreen Cove Holistic Health Center (full text presented in the appendix) |
| Chapter 3: Focusing the Evaluation Using Appreciative Inquiry | 3 | Evaluating the training provided by the New Mexico Coalition of Sexual Assault Programs (CSAP) |
| | 4 | Evaluating a two-year Appreciative Inquiry initiative of an alternative health center |
| | 5 | Evaluating knowledge sharing and capacity building in education for the World Bank |
| Chapter 4: Designing and Conducting Interviews and Surveys Using Appreciative Inquiry | 6 | Conducting phone interviews to evaluate the training provided by a state education agency |
| | 7 | The impact of using one appreciative question to evaluate a city health department |
| | 8 | Conducting focus groups to evaluate the Girl Scouts Beyond Bars program |

*(Continued)*

(Continued)

# Preface

We are passionate about evaluation . . . and because we feel strongly about the value of evaluation and the critical role it can play in organizations, we continually seek ways to improve our practice and make evaluation more meaningful, useful, and relevant for today's changing and volatile organizational environments. Because organizations are never stagnant and are constantly responding both to internal and external stimuli and pressures, evaluators must continuously scan the environments in which they work so that they can identify and respond in ways that maximize an evaluation's effectiveness and usefulness.

Although we have each come to Appreciative Inquiry (AI) from different places, our varied experiences have confirmed and reaffirmed the power of using an appreciative approach for understanding and improving an organization's programs, processes, products, policies, and systems. As an organizational development and change strategy, AI often has a profound influence on the way people think and act. By helping organization members envision a future based on past successes, AI is able to energize and motivate them to strive for more peak experiences because they know they are possible. Used within an evaluation context, Appreciative Inquiry offers evaluators another way to focus an evaluation, to design interview guides and surveys, to develop evaluation systems, and ultimately to develop an organization's evaluation capacity. AI helps participants see the possibilities of evaluation.

Our interest in writing this book stems from our conviction that AI offers evaluators another means for framing and conducting evaluations. It is not a replacement for other evaluation approaches, nor is it a panacea for many of the challenges that evaluators face. Rather, we suggest that Appreciative Inquiry offers evaluators at least two options—it may be simply understood and used as one more evaluation method, approach, or strategy, or it may be viewed and used more ambitiously as a means for challenging the foundations of evaluation practice by shifting evaluation from something that can, at best, produce incremental positive changes, to something that can generate exponential, radical changes in organizations and communities.

Our primary goal was to write a book that included detailed explanations and illustrations of how to apply Appreciative Inquiry in evaluation practice. We wanted to make Appreciative Inquiry accessible and to invite our readers to include Appreciative Inquiry in their repertoire of evaluation knowledge, skills, and tools.

## Organization of This Book

We think of this book as a *crossover* book—in particular, a bridge between evaluation and organizational development and change. While crossovers are often seen in the music world, where a rock singer makes a jazz recording, or a jazz performer makes a classical recording, this book represents our attempt to appeal to evaluators, organization development consultants, managers, program staff, researchers, and others who work in corporate, nonprofit, education, government, and healthcare organizations—essentially, anyone interested in evaluative inquiry.

We begin the book with a Prologue that invites the reader to approach Appreciative Inquiry through a story of an evaluator named Ben who decides to try AI in his evaluation. Alongside Ben, we invite you to be intrigued with the experience and to join us in exploring the application of Appreciative Inquiry to evaluation. Because using AI in evaluation practice represents a paradigmatic shift—a reframing of how we can design and implement an evaluation—we ask readers to remain open to exploring new ways of thinking as they read through the different chapters.

For those new to Appreciative Inquiry, Chapter 1 provides a detailed discussion of AI's history, processes, and uses within the organizational development and change arena. For those unfamiliar with or new to evaluation as a profession and discipline, Chapter 2 orients the reader to definitions of evaluation, similarities between Appreciative Inquiry and evaluation, and examples of how AI has been used for evaluation purposes, as well as the benefits of using Appreciative Inquiry in evaluation.

Chapters 3, 4, and 5 describe specific applications of AI to evaluation. In Chapter 3, we describe how AI processes can be used to focus an evaluation study—to determine an evaluation's purpose, stakeholders, key questions, and design and data collection methods. How to reframe and design interview guides and surveys using appreciative questions is the focus of Chapter 4. And, in Chapter 5, we discuss how to use Appreciative Inquiry to develop an organization's evaluation system. In each of these three chapters, case examples illustrate the various applications of AI in an evaluation context.

A major premise of the book is that the use of Appreciative Inquiry for evaluative purposes ultimately builds an organization's evaluation capacity. Chapter 6 shows how engaging in an AI process that is evaluation-focused increases participants' understanding of and commitment to evaluation, enriches the evaluation experience through whole-systems thinking, increases the culture-competence of the evaluation, and deepens participants' learning experience through evaluation.

We conclude the book with an Epilogue in which we address the challenges in truly embracing an affirmative and strengths-based approach to evaluation. We emphasize that by crossing boundaries—by going beyond traditional methods of evaluation—the evaluation profession and discipline will be more enriched, effective, and valued; and, most importantly, it will be more relevant to today's ever-changing and interconnected organizational and social issues.

While each of these chapters could be read separately, we recommend that Chapters 1 and 2 be read prior to the remaining chapters so that the reader understands the foundational principles of both AI and evaluation, and is clear about the authors' perspectives and assumptions about both forms of inquiry.

## Audiences for This Book

Our hope is that anyone who designs, conducts, administers, or oversees evaluation activities and studies will benefit from this book. These audiences include, but are not limited to

- Trainers and instructors of evaluation workshops and courses

- Evaluators and consultants who work in the nonprofit sector, which is increasingly trying to define evaluation approaches that work within the "culture of philanthropy" and have been most attracted to assets-based and strengths-based approaches

- Evaluators and consultants who conduct evaluations in cultures that value storytelling

- Managers of evaluation who want evaluations that are constructive and less threatening

- Evaluators and consultants who have been exposed to Appreciative Inquiry and other assets-based approaches and are curious about how to apply it to their work

- Evaluators, consultants, and managers who are looking for new ways to address old problems and want to increase the usefulness and meaningfulness of evaluation

- Organization development consultants who wish to better understand how to apply Appreciative Inquiry within an evaluation context

- Managers who are seeking new ways to engage staff in responding to new and persistent issues

# Acknowledgments

This book has been a labor of love. However, love alone does not get the job done; there are several individuals to whom we are very grateful. In particular, we would like to thank Michael Quinn Patton, who has provided ongoing support of this project. He is one of the most professionally generous people we have ever met. A warm thank-you goes to Laverne D. Webb, EnCompass CEO, an Appreciative Inquiry guru who, in 1997, provided the inspiration and coaching for many who were just beginning to use AI in evaluation contexts. We want to thank Ana Coghlan who, through her belief in the value of AI and its application to evaluation, brought us together early in our collaboration—to her, we are sincerely grateful. We are also indebted to Lisa Cuevas Shaw, our good-natured, patient, and caring editor, who immediately saw the potential for applying Appreciative Inquiry to evaluation. Her stewardship and belief in this book empowered us to bring this work to fruition.

When we first conceptualized this book, we knew that it would be critically important to include case examples that would help readers understand what applying Appreciative Inquiry to evaluation looks like. To make this happen, we called upon several of our colleagues and clients for permission to include their stories about using AI. We would like to offer a special note of thanks to (in alphabetical order) Kim Alaburda, Joe Amon, Maria Borrero, Bruno Bouchet, Jim Buford, Arlette Campbell White, Nancy Coen, William Dudeck, Diane Dunet, William Eckert, Bob Hyman, Stephane Legros, Tobias Linden, Rashad Massoud, Juan Manuel Moreno, Dave Nicholas, Karen Norum, Patti Poindexter, Sherry Rockey, Dawn Smart, Anne Thomas, Teresa Tidwell, Tamara Walser, and Marcy Wells, for their graciousness and support of this book.

We also want to thank those who have worked hard to define, describe, and practice Appreciative Inquiry, and who have made their work so available to others. Some of those who stand out for us include David Cooperrider, Diana Whitney, Charles Elliott, Jane Watkins, Bernard Mohr, Mac Odell, Jim Ludema, Sheila McNamee, Ron Fry, Amanda Trosten-Bloom, Jackie Stavros, and Ken Gergen. Their writings and workshops have enabled many to understand and use Appreciative Inquiry in a wide variety of organizational and community contexts.

Finally, we are very grateful to Gail Johnson, Mac Odell, and Michael Q. Patton, who reviewed an earlier draft of this manuscript. Their support, belief in our work, and thoughtful and insightful suggestions helped clarify many of the ideas and practices described in this book.

We hope that this book inspires, provokes, and encourages those involved in evaluation practice to consider the possibilities of using Appreciative Inquiry to reframe their evaluation work.

*Beliefs influence perception.*
*Perception structures reality.*
*Reality suggests possibilities.*
*Possibilities generate choices.*
*Choices initiate actions.*
*Actions affect outcomes.*
*Outcomes impact beliefs . . .*
*Awareness facilitates change.*
*Change anywhere becomes change*
*Everywhere.*

—Tobin Quereau, 1994

# Prologue

## *Choosing an Evaluation Path*

Miranda and Ben work for Evaluation, Inc., a 20-person evaluation consulting firm. They have recently begun an evaluation of a Department of Health's service quality and client satisfaction. The evaluation was commissioned in response to the negative publicity the department has been receiving in the media. In particular, news stories have highlighted the department's inability to address the needs of the poor and underserved in the state, its non-responsiveness to Medicaid patients, and its seeming disinterest in being accountable to its constituents.

In collaboration with their boss, Marietta, and several departmental staff, Miranda and Ben develop an evaluation plan that describes a two-phase evaluation process. The plan includes background information on the department's services, a list of stakeholders, key evaluation questions, data collection and analysis methods, a timeline, and a budget. The first phase of the evaluation is to gather data from the department's internal staff. Depending on these findings, phase two will be implemented with a sample of the department's clients. One of the data collection methods they have chosen to use in phase one is telephone interviews. Based on the evaluation's key questions, Miranda and Ben decide to design an interview guide that includes questions concerning the staff's roles and responsibilities, how the department functions, how information is communicated internally and externally, how decisions are made, how they receive feedback on their work performance, and how that feedback is incorporated into their decisions for improved services.

Ben has just heard about an approach he wants to try in the interviews—it's called Appreciative Inquiry. However, Miranda does not think this is the time to be trying something new. After some discussion with Marietta, they get approval to conduct the interviews using two different interview guides (approaches), and to compare the data obtained from each one. The following are the two interview guides:

| Miranda's Interview Guide | Ben's Interview Guide |
|---|---|
| Good morning. This is Miranda B. from Evaluation, Inc., the company conducting an evaluation of the Department of Health's quality of service. As indicated earlier in our request to talk with you, this interview will take approximately 30 minutes. Your responses will be confidential—your name will not be used in reporting the results of this evaluation. | Good morning. This is Ben M. from Evaluation, Inc., the company conducting an evaluation of the Department of Health's quality of service. As indicated earlier in our request to talk with you, this interview will take approximately 30 minutes. Your responses will be confidential— your name will not be used in reporting the results of this evaluation. |

Your name:

1. What is your job title?
2. What are your main responsibilities?
3. Who do you report to?
4. Do you have a job description? If yes, may I see a copy of it?
5. How often does your supervisor communicate with you?
6. Do you feel that this communication is adequate? (Ask for examples.)
7. What decisions are you authorized to make on your own?
8. When you need approval, what is the process you follow to get approval?
9. How long does it take to get such approvals—are decisions made in a timely fashion?
10. How do you receive feedback on the quality of the services you provide?
11. If you receive feedback, how do you use it?
12. Do you have any other comments?

Thank you for your time.

Your name:

1. What is your job title?
2. What are your main responsibilities?
3. Do you have a job description? If yes, may I see a copy of it?
4. I would like you to think about a time when, as a staff member in this department, you had an exceptional experience—when you were most proud of being here doing this work. You knew that you were making a difference in the lives of people you were serving. Think back and tell me a story about this experience.
5. What made this exceptional experience possible?
6. What did you do to make it possible? Who else contributed to it?
7. What decisions led to this exceptional experience? How were these decisions made?
8. What feedback from your supervisor and others was most useful in making this experience possible?
9. What do you most value about the work you do?
10. What do you most value about this department?
11. If you could make three wishes for this department so that you could have more of these exceptional experiences, what would they be?

I really enjoyed hearing about your experiences. Thank you for sharing these with me.

Miranda is concerned that Ben's interview guide is too broad and will fail to address the evaluation's key questions. Ben believes that using the appreciative approach will be more effective at illuminating the "real" issues. In addition, he explains that if, for some reason, the interviewees' responses do not address the main evaluation topics, he will ask about these directly to make sure that the evaluation questions are answered. Ben also thinks this approach will be more productive since the staff's morale has been low since the department began receiving the negative press. He senses that this type of questioning will encourage the staff to be more forthcoming in their responses and that the resulting data will be more useful.

At the end of the first day of interviews, Miranda and Ben get together to debrief. Miranda explains that she spoke with six staff members. She complains, however, that, by the end of the sixth interview, she was drained and angry at the incompetence she learned about. There were no job descriptions in sight, there were no formal feedback loops, and the staff seemed apathetic, not caring about performance or customer service. She also felt uncertain about how decisions were actually being made, and wanted to get more information so she could develop a variety of decision-making flow charts.

Ben also interviewed six people. His interviews took a little longer than Miranda's, but he says that he came away energized and amazed at what the staff had been accomplishing under such difficult conditions. He heard stories about staff who had spent their own money to buy disinfectants that could be used to clean community health clinics; he heard about staff who went out of their way to make coalitions happen and make funding available to serve those in need, and about staff who went beyond the call of duty helping out in crises when there was a shortage of personnel. From these stories, he has documented ineffective work processes, examples of how staff invented creative methods to provide good service in spite of significant obstacles, the staff's need to have greater direction from management, and how they developed ways to provide client feedback to the department.

While Miranda was drained, Ben was energized. While Miranda felt stonewalled, Ben felt trusted. While Miranda felt like she was stuck on the worst possible project, Ben felt hopeful about producing a constructive and useful evaluation report. Miranda and Ben's use of different interviewing approaches led them down very different paths, and as a result, they were exposed to very different realities that existed in the same organization. While Miranda chose to study problems and gaps in the organization as a way of learning about its performance, Ben chose to study successes or peak experiences. Both Miranda and Ben learned about the organization's problems, but only Ben saw how things worked when they worked well. While Miranda saw a static picture of problems and gaps, Ben saw a fluid, constantly adapting, dynamic system.

The choice of language and perspective is at the heart of what it means to apply Appreciative Inquiry to evaluation. We can choose to see the glass as half empty or half full, and by our choice, we begin to co-construct the reality we see. It is not "I will believe when I see," but "I will see when I believe." Miranda went into this work looking to identify and document gaps and to make recommendations; Ben went into the same work looking to identify successes and to discover what is getting in the way of people's dreams and hopes. Both Ben and Miranda wanted to benefit from the rich qualitative data that interviews can produce, but they asked very different kinds of questions. Consequently, the staff provided very different types of evaluative information.

This book represents a theory to practice philosophy and approach. As such, we will look at the ideas that guided Miranda's and Ben's choices, and illustrate how to apply Appreciative Inquiry to evaluation carefully and deliberately. It invites evaluators to explore how the sincere and systematic study of success can lead them to discoveries about goals, desired outcomes, indicators, evaluation use, and recommendations for improvement. The book aims to expand the evaluator's thinking and toolkit and to become a guidebook for immediate application of this approach. The reader will benefit most from this book by following Ben's example of staying open and curious about how AI can contribute to effective evaluation practice. If, after reading this book, you integrate Appreciative Inquiry into your evaluation repertoire, we would be most pleased to hear of your experiences, questions, and thoughts.

*Every day you may make progress. Every step may be fruitful. Yet there will stretch out before you an ever-lengthening, ever-ascending, ever-improving path. You know you will never get to the end of the journey. But this, so far from discouraging, only adds to the joy and glory of the climb.*

—Winston Churchill (British orator, author, and prime minister during World War II, 1874–1965)

# Introducing Appreciative Inquiry  1

*The only real voyage of discovery exists, not in seeing new land-scapes, but in having new eyes.*

—Marcel Proust

Asking questions is fundamental to organizational learning, growth, change, renewal, and success. The kinds of questions we think matter most are those that are learning oriented—questions that challenge our assumptions, affirm each others' strengths and gifts, help us reflect on past successful experiences, foster creativity and innovation, and stimulate curiosity and excitement. For organizations and communities to move forward, to reach their goals in an unpredictable and chaotic world, it is critical that we begin to ask more questions. The questions that will help us achieve our future are not those that accuse, find fault, and condemn, but those that create energy, hope, and motivation. This chapter introduces the reader to an organizational development and change process called Appreciative Inquiry (AI). In addition to describing the history and underlying assumptions, principles, and practices of Appreciative Inquiry, it includes two case examples of how AI has been applied to designing and facilitating organizational development and change.

## Defining Appreciative Inquiry

Appreciative Inquiry is a group process that inquires into, identifies, and further develops the best of "what is" in organizations in order to create a better future. Often used in the organization development field as an approach to large-scale change, it is a means for addressing issues, challenges, changes, and concerns of an organization in ways that build on the successful, effective, and energizing experiences of its members. Underlying AI is a belief that the questions we ask are critical to the world we create. In so doing, "organizations move toward what they study" (Cooperrider, Whitney, & Stavros, 2003, p. 29). As Watkins and Cooperrider (2000) explain, Appreciative Inquiry

> seeks what is "right" in an organization. It is a habit of mind, heart, and imagination that searches for the success, the life-giving force, the incidence of joy. It moves toward what the organization is doing right and provides a frame for creating an imagined future that builds on and expands the joyful and life-giving realities as the metaphor and organizing principle of the organization. (p. 6)

Thus, AI is both a philosophy and a process for creating the kinds of organizations in which people want to work, and a world in which they wish to live (Watkins & Mohr, 2001). As an organizational change approach, however, Appreciative Inquiry addresses organizational issues in a significantly different way. Instead of focusing on problems and what is not working and why, Appreciative Inquiry asks organization members first to discover what is working particularly well and then to envision what it might be like if "the best of what is" occurred more frequently. Based on their images of *what can be* that are born from *the best of what was*, organization members design and implement the desired changes. As Whitney and Trosten-Bloom (2003) note, "Appreciative Inquiry borrows from the strengths of many other practices in the field of organization development" (p. 10). These include Open Space Technology (an approach to self-organizing), whole scale change (facilitating large-scale meetings), organizational learning (valuing inquiry, dialogue, and reflection), and Future Search (bringing stakeholders together to create the future). Yet, Whitney and Trosten-Bloom propose that AI is distinctly different from other organization development approaches because it is (a) fully affirmative, (b) inquiry-based, and (c) improvisational (p. 10).

Since the late 1980s, Appreciative Inquiry has been used in a wide variety of organizations and for many different purposes. It has been applied to strategic planning, culture transformation, increasing customer satisfaction, organization redesign, and leadership development. It has also been used to integrate organizations after a merger, to build alliances and union-management partnerships, for peace building, and for implementing educational reform and economic development efforts (Whitney & Trosten-Bloom, 2003). Appreciative Inquiry has also been used to help organizations improve more effectively through "discovery and valuing, envisioning, dialogue and co-constructing the future" (Ashford & Patkar, 2001, p. 4). Furthermore, AI supports generative learning within organizations—learning that "emphasizes continuous experimentation, systematic rather than fragmented thinking, and a willingness to think outside the accepted limitations of a problem" (Barrett, 1995, p. 36). This learning culture enables organization members to challenge underlying assumptions, raise fundamental questions regarding organizational life, and reframe what has been taken for granted (van der Haar & Hosking, 2004).

To understand better why Appreciative Inquiry is successful, Whitney and Trosten-Bloom (2003) interviewed people who had participated in AI workshops and activities. The data from their interviews indicated six reasons why Appreciative Inquiry works (pp. 20–21):

1. It builds relationships enabling people to be known in relationship, rather than in role.

2. It creates an opportunity for people to be heard.

3. It generates opportunities for people to dream and to share their dreams.

4. It creates an environment in which people are able to choose how they contribute.

5. It gives people both discretion and the support to act.

6. It encourages and enables people to be positive.

What makes AI unique as an organizational development and change process is its attention to (a) being purposefully positive, (b) building on past successes, (c) emphasizing a grass roots and top down approach, (d) being highly participative, (e) stimulating vision and creativity, and (f) accelerating change (Cooperrider & Whitney, 2002). Not wanting to dismiss all problem-focused approaches to change, Whitney and Trosten-Bloom (2003) explain, "in our experience, deficit-based change can work—it has for years, just not as effectively as positive change" (p. 16).

As the definitions of the words *appreciate* and *inquiry* imply, Appreciative Inquiry is about recognizing the best in people; acknowledging those things that give life; affirming past and present strengths, successes, assets, and potentials; and asking questions, studying, and searching, exploring, and investigating.

## A Movement Toward Appreciative Language

The words we use in our normal daily discourse matter. How and what we choose to communicate reflects not only how we think and behave, but it also affects how those around us respond to what we say. According to Elliott (1999), "what the appreciative approach seeks to achieve is the transformation of a culture from one that sees itself in largely negative terms—and therefore *is inclined to become locked in its own negative construction of itself*—to one that sees itself as having within it the capacity to enrich and enhance the quality of life of all the stakeholders—*and therefore moves toward this appreciative construction of itself*" (p. 12; emphasis in the original). The negative terms to which Elliott refers are reflected in the deficit-based vocabularies that are often used in our personal and professional lives. For example, the language frequently used to describe organizational deficits includes *organizational stress, work alienation, role conflict, defensive routines, bureaucratic red tape, turfism, groupthink, burnout, neurotic,* and *dysfunctional organization.* Words to describe human deficit include *depressed, anti-social, paranoid, mid-life crisis, controlling, obsessive-compulsive, anal,* and *identity crisis.* Appreciative Inquiry practitioners believe that this language not only creates images that restrict creativity, hope, and success, but that if you look at problems, you tend to find and create more problems. Conversely, if you look for success, you are more likely to find and create more success.

In search of a more productive and effective way to work with students, clients, customers, colleagues, and community members, various professions have eschewed the use of deficit-based language where terms such as *broken, dysfunctional, sick, problem, defensive, disability, neurotic, incompetent,* and *burnout* are used to describe why things are the way they are, or why things will not change. As a result, interest in asset-based and strengths-based approaches to addressing issues in communities and organizations has been increasing over the last several years. The following are some examples.

### Community Development

The field of community development has been adopting an asset-based approach to its work for several years. John Kretzmann, of The Asset-Based Community Development Institute based at Northwestern University's Institute for Policy Research, believes that the focus on identifying community needs in the last few decades has been costly, ineffective, and even counterproductive. Kretzmann and McKnight (1996) suggest that people working with community development projects have taken one of two paths. The first path has focused on determining a community's needs, deficiencies, and problems. This path, they say, has been the "most traveled." The second path—one that they strongly advocate—focuses on "beginning with a clear commitment to discovering a community's capacities and assets" (p. 23). Kretzmann and McKnight suggest that the first path has led to the development of a language of deficit, which in turn has led to a plethora of deficiency-based policies and programs. As a result of the underlying assumptions of problem-focused services, community residents begin to see themselves as "people with special needs that can only be met by outsiders" (p. 23), thus further enabling the "dependency syndrome" that often characterizes such systems. However, using an asset-based approach empowers communities to make the most of what is working well and helps them allocate new and existing resources more effectively. As Kretzmann and McKnight explain, "This community development strategy starts with what is present in the community, the capacities of its residents and workers, the associational and institutional base of the area," and builds on the relationships already in place in the community (p. 27). An asset-based approach also acknowledges that not all communities are the same—that each has different strengths and interests and thus different strategies will work with different communities based on their internal interests and capacities.

Asset-based approaches recognize the value of the social capital present in relationships and interactions between community groups and individuals. An example of such an asset-based community development effort is The Connecticut Assets Network (CAN; http://www.ctassets.org/about/index.cfm), a grassroots nonprofit network of citizens that promotes the integration and successful use of asset-based strategies to community development. The organization believes that community members should be networking and engaging in conversations "to develop asset-rich relationships where people discover their many gifts, talents, and capacities for mutually beneficial problem solving." To emphasize the importance of asset-based language as a foundational principle, CAN has developed a vision, mission, values, and goals that illustrate the affirmative philosophy that guides their work (see Figure 1.1).

Asset-based community development is based on a belief that individuals have had many difficult experiences and, as a result, have summoned a variety of resources to survive and even thrive.

## Social Work

Similar to the asset-based approach to community development is the strengths perspective being applied in the social work field. According to Roff (2004),

> The strengths perspective encompasses an approach to social work practice that emphasizes the strengths and resources of people and their environments, rather than their problems and pathologies . . . with its emphasis on fostering the innate problem-solving capacities of individuals, families and communities, [a strengths perspective] provides social workers with a framework that moves away from pathology and towards development and growth. (pp. 203–204)

**Vision:**

The Connecticut Assets Network envisions people living in communities where *everyone is a resource and makes a difference.*

**Mission:**

The Connecticut Assets Network promotes the integration and successful use of asset-based strategies to build healthier communities, where people discover and share their many gifts, talents, and capacities.

**Values:**

*We believe:*

- Communities support neighbors in meeting and respectfully working with one another.
- Neighbors participate in discovering each other's abilities (connectedness).
- Individuals, associations, and institutions contribute time and abilities in supporting and caring for their community (cohesiveness).
- Local partnerships promote responsibility in decision making and community building.
- Business, government, faith, and nonprofit organizations advance integrity in local governing boards.

**Goals:**

*Leadership:* To develop local and state leadership in the area of asset-based community development.

*Resources:* To develop asset-rich relationships locally that result in connections for mutually beneficial support and community building.

*Strategies:* To integrate strategies that promote community connectedness/cohesiveness resulting in citizen development and contribution as the foundation for sustained solutions to challenges.

*Education:* To promote accountability to funders and communities through tracking outcomes that leads to participatory planning.

**Figure 1.1**    Connecticut Assets Network Vision, Mission, Values, and Goals

In 1992, Saleebey published what has become a widely referenced book on the topic of using a strengths perspective in social work. In this book he and others argue that the majority of social work theories are filled with the language of pathology and problems, which only reinforces individuals' low self-perceptions of worth and dignity. As Cohen (1999) explains, this can become, or feed, a self-fulfilling prophecy.

> To refer to a human being as a paraplegic, a manic-depressive, an unmarried mother, an addict, an offender, a borderline personality, a sexual psychopath, a bag lady, a pre-orgasmic or a post-traumatic is to elevate the deficit of deviance to the status of dominant identity of that person. (p. 461)

According to Saleebey (1992), the strengths perspective in social work is based on a core set of ideas and themes that include empowerment, membership, regeneration, synergy, dialogue, and suspension of belief.

Implementing this philosophy shifts the social worker's efforts "from professional work as the exerting of the power of knowledge and/or institution to professional work as collaborating with the power within the individual (or community) toward a life that is palpably better, and better in the client's own terms" (p. 13). The critical point here is that the future and how to achieve it is determined by what has worked for the individual client based on his or her own strengths and assets, and not by someone who knows little of that person's lived experiences or context.

Those who work in the mental health and social service arena are also using a strengths-based philosophy and approach in their work. Powell and Batsche (1997) explain that traditional models of human services have been based on an expert identifying and treating an individual's problem and then recommending a treatment to restore the individual to a normalized state. They write, "sometimes referred to as deficit models, traditional approaches were characterized by paternalistic values and hierarchical behaviors in which things were done 'for' or 'to' clients" (p. 2). However, using a strength-based approach focuses instead on

> the unique knowledge, competencies, capabilities, and resources of individual family members as well as the family as a whole . . . a strength-based philosophy does not focus on the past or place blame on the parent or family for causing problems. A different approach to problem solving is utilized—one that asks what strategies and resources families currently use to solve problems and that seeks to build the family's capacity to resolve current problems and minimize future ones. (p. 3)

## Education

Strengths-based approaches are also being applied within K–12 schools. For example, in an alternative middle and high school setting with chronically disruptive students, Carpenter-Aeby and Kurtz (2000) found that a strengths-based portfolio assessment "provided a framework to organize educational and social interventions for students to take responsibility for their actions, for students and families to create new healthy narratives for school and home, and for documenting students' hard work" (p. 229). Those who work with school populations argue that for too long youth have been treated "as 'predators,' their families 'dysfunctional,' their communities as 'blighted'" (Osher, 1996, p. 26). It is no wonder, Osher says, that many of our interventions fail. He believes that deficit-oriented approaches that lead to "victim-blaming" only serve to reinforce research, policies, and practices that focus on deficiencies. In the end, the use of such language isolates "the client and the problem from the context in which the problem developed" (p. 27). Many are beginning to advocate that assets-based and strengths-based approaches serve as a foundation of hope, and only with that hope can we then "look at communities as more than a nest of problems" and implement interventions that work (p. 28).

### Positive Organizational Scholarship

A movement within the organizational and social sciences called *Positive Organizational Scholarship* is also focusing on how an affirmative stance influences and guides individual and organizational behavior. Cameron and Caza (2004) explain that

> Positive Organizational Scholarship (POS) focuses on the dynamics leading to exceptional individual and organizational performance such as developing human strength, producing resilience and restoration, and fostering vitality. . . . POS investigates positive deviance, or the ways in which organizations and their members flourish and prosper in especially favorable ways. (p. 731)

While Positive Organizational Scholarship involves studying positive phenomena, it "does not ignore the presence of negative, challenging, or contrary aspects of organizations" (p. 731). Rather, this approach seeks "to study organizations and organizational contexts typified by appreciation, collaboration, vitality, and fulfillment, where creating abundance and human well-being are key indicators of success. It seeks to understand what represents the best of the human condition in organizations" (Cameron, Dutton, Quinn, & Spreitzer, 2004). Ludema, Wilmot, and Srivastva (1997) further suggest that "the purpose of social and organizational science ought to be to create *textured vocabularies of hope*—stories, theories, evidence, and illustrations— that provide humanity with new guiding images of relational possibility" (p. 1016; emphasis in the original). Those who take a positive approach to studying organizations address a wide variety of organizational issues. They include research on organizational design and structures, leadership, organizational change, work design, organizational errors and tragedies, social networks, and community building (Cameron & Caza, 2004).

Interests in positive and affirmative ways of knowing are not new, nor are they unique. The examples presented above illustrate a growing interest and commitment to using assets-based and strengths-based approaches to inquiry in several different disciplines. In the next section we describe the origins of Appreciative Inquiry and the theories on which it is based.

## Origins of Appreciative Inquiry

Appreciative Inquiry was born out of the doctoral work of David Cooperrider in 1980 when, as a student at Case Western Reserve University, he began his research focused on the question, "What's wrong with the human side of the organization?" As he conducted his interviews he "was amazed by the level of positive cooperation, innovation and egalitarian governance in the organization" (Watkins & Mohr, 2001, p. 15). He found that when he asked questions that were problem focused, people lost energy and became less engaged with the interview. However, when he asked about why things succeeded, the interviewees' level of interest and energy increased. The power of this finding caused Cooperrider to shift his focus to analyzing the factors that were contributing to the effective functioning of the organization (in this instance, The Cleveland Clinic). The term *Appreciative Inquiry* was first used only as a footnote in the feedback report to the clinic. However, "the report creates such a powerful and positive stir that the Board calls for ways to use this method with the whole group practice" (Watkins & Mohr, p. 16). Cooperrider completed his doctoral dissertation in 1986 and in it he presented a set of AI principles, AI logic, and four AI phases (Discovery, Dream, Design, Destiny). He then began to present and write about his findings and approach in a variety of venues.

In 1990, Cooperrider along with Diana Whitney, Ken and Mary Gergen, Sheila McNamee, Harlene Anderson, and Suresh Srivastva (Cooperrider's dissertation advisor) founded the Taos Institute (http://www.taosinstitute .com), which hosts workshops on Appreciative Inquiry and related topics, and publishes books on dialogue, social constructionist thinking, and social change. During the 1990s Cooperrider and others facilitated several large-scale Appreciative Inquiry Summits throughout the world, and published several books on AI. In 1997, the AI listserv was initiated, and it currently serves as a forum for AI practitioners to share their experiences and lessons learned (see the Appreciative Inquiry Commons at http://appreciativeinquiry.case.edu for how to access this listserv). And, by the end of the 1990s, an electronic AI newsletter had been launched (*AI Practitioner,* http://www.aipractitioner.com). Over the last few years several books and articles have been published on AI, an increasing number of presentations describing how AI has been used in a multitude of contexts have been made at professional conferences, and numerous workshops on AI have been offered around the world.

## Core Principles and Underlying Assumptions of Appreciative Inquiry

AI researchers and practitioners have developed eight principles that serve as the foundation for understanding how Appreciative Inquiry is implemented, and why so many believe it works. Although Cooperrider identified the first five of these principles in his original work, the addition of principles six through eight are evidence of the continuing evolution of this approach (Cooperrider, Whitney, & Stavros, 2003; Watkins & Mohr, 2001; Whitney & Trosten-Bloom, 2003).

1. **The Constructionist Principle:** Social knowledge and organizational destiny are interwoven. This means that reality "is constructed during the social interactions of people, rather than in the mind of the individual" (Watkins & Mohr, 2001, p. 195), and that knowledge is an evolving construct that is shaped by the experiences and conversations we have with each other. As such, the language we use, and the relationships we have with each other, create our future.

2. **The Principle of Simultaneity:** Inquiry and change are not separate; they can and should be simultaneous. All forms of inquiry should be thought of as interventions. As soon as individuals ask questions and engage in conversation, they may begin to change the way they think and act. Thus, the questions one asks set the stage for what is found and what is discovered. These data form the stories in which the future is conceived, discussed, and constructed.

3. **The Poetic Principle:** Human organizations are open books—endless sources of learning, inspiration, and interpretation. An organization's story is continually being co-authored by the people within it as well as by those outside who interact with it; it is like a narrative, a grand story, co-authored by its various stakeholders. We can choose what we study in an organization—the choice of the inquiry influences the direction of the organization.

4. **The Anticipatory Principle:** The most important resources we have for generating constructive organizational change or improvements are our collective imagination and our discourse about the future. That is, our image of the future is what will guide us in determining how we will achieve the future. The more positive and hopeful the image of the future, the more positive the present-day action.

5. **The Positive Principle:** Momentum for change requires large amounts of positive affect and social bonding, attitudes such as hope, inspiration, and the sheer joy of creating with one another. People and organizations move in the direction of their inquiries—positive image results in positive action.

6. **The Wholeness Principle:** Wholeness brings out the best in people and organizations. Involving all of the stakeholders in a large group process stimulates creativity and builds a collective capacity. It is related to understanding the whole story, engaging with the whole system, and sharing one's whole person.

7. **The Enactment Principle:** To really make a change, we must "be the change we want to see." Positive change occurs when we have a model of the ideal future and are living examples of this future. We must be fully present and live the way we want to be. The future is now. We create it in the moment with our words, images, and relationships.

8. **The Free Choice Principle:** People perform better and are more committed when they have the freedom to choose how and what they contribute. Free choice stimulates organizational excellence and positive change and liberates both personal and organizational power.

As Whitney and Trosten-Bloom (2003) write, "taken together, the eight principles of Appreciative Inquiry point to one simple message—Appreciative Inquiry is about conversations that matter" (p. 78). Summarizing these principles, Hammond (1996, pp. 20–21) offers the following:

- In every society, organization, or group, something works.
- What we focus on becomes our reality.
- Reality is created in the moment, and there are multiple realities.
- The act of asking questions of an organization or group influences the group in some way.
- People have more confidence and comfort to journey to the future (the unknown) when they carry forward parts of the past (the known).
- If we carry parts of the past forward, they should be what are best about the past.
- It is important to value differences.
- The language we use creates our reality.

These eight principles are born out of several theories and related research studies that have focused on the effects of positive image and positive thinking. First is the *placebo effect,* which has been an area of significant study in the medical field ever since researcher H. K. Beecher published his paper, "The Powerful Placebo," in 1955. After analyzing data from 26 studies, Beecher concluded that 32% of the patients had responded to a placebo. Described as the measurable, observable, or felt improvement in health not attributable to the treatment, the placebo effect has been subject to a great deal of interest. The effect has typically been studied in situations where one group of individuals was provided real medication and a control group was given a sugar or dummy pill or other "fake" therapy. Many studies have found that between 35%–75% of the patients who received the placebo felt better, or their medical condition improved. Increasingly, researchers are suggesting that the placebo effect is a result of both psychological and physiological factors. Providing that "the mind is a product of the brain, and the brain and the body are intimately connected by a network of nerves and by hormones and other molecules that mediate any physiological functions," it is possible that one's beliefs (or mind-set) stimulate changes in one's neurochemistry, which, in turn, produces a change in one's physical being (Groopman,

2004, p. 163). For example, some researchers are finding that the anticipatory reality that occurs through suggestion plays a central role in how one responds to certain stimuli. And some have found that when sick people are shown care, compassion, and affection, it triggers a physical reaction in the body, which then prompts healing (Talbot, 2000).

Related to the placebo effect is the well-known and highly researched phenomenon called the *Pygmalion effect,* which is often referred to as the "self-fulfilling prophecy." Put simply, the Pygmalion effect reflects the idea that what we expect to happen will happen when we have certain expectations that are projected onto another person. Although the origin of this social construct began with Merton (1948) and was considered by educational researchers in the 1950s and early 1960s, the phenomenon struck a chord with the now classic 1968 Pygmalion study by Rosenthal and Jacobsen. In their research conducted at the "Oak School," they tested the non-verbal IQ of students in grades 1–6 and randomly labeled 20% of them as "intellectual bloomers" to their teachers. The students were again tested at the end of the year. The researchers' "results indicated strongly that children from whom teachers expected greater intellectual gains showed such gains" (Rosenthal & Jacobsen, 1968, p. 184). This meant that the teachers developed positive or negative images of their students that translated into expectations for their students' performance. Of course, what the teachers didn't know was that the students had been randomly assigned to one of the two treatment groups, and all of the student groups were equivalent in terms of their potential performance. Set against the backdrop of the 1960s and with great concerns about the education of minority students, the research was lauded and highly publicized. Over the next 17 years, however, more than 300 reports were published that discussed, critiqued, and reviewed Rosenthal and Jacobsen's work (Meyer, 1985). While many of the criticisms were well founded, most agree that the Pygmalion effect does exist in educational settings, although it is a much more complicated concept than originally thought.

While research on the idea of self-fulfilling prophecy was being conducted in schools, it was also being studied in work settings. Several studies have focused on how subordinates' performance is influenced by their managers' expectations (Berlew & Hall, 1966; Livingston, 1969). Study after study has supported the concept of the Pygmalion effect by illustrating that when employees are perceived to be low performers or to have less developed skills, they tend to perform in a manner consistent with these expectations.

A corollary to both the placebo and the Pygmalion effects is the concept of *positive images.* For example, Cooperrider et al. (2003) point out that various Western civilization scholars have noted that the "fundamental images held by a civilization or culture have an enormous influence on its fate . . . when there is a vision or a bright image of the future, the people flourish" (p. 11–12). Often referred to as the heliotropic principle, the underlying assumption of positive images is that organizations operate like plants; they move toward what gives them life and energy, similar to how sunflowers grow toward the sun (Elliott, 1999). As a result, organizations and communities grow toward the images they hold. Thus, if organizations and communities share positive images of their future, they will be able to develop the programs, policies, processes, systems, and products to achieve that future.

The notion of positive images also plays a role in the *narrative of stories* that people share in organizations and communities. It is through the stories people tell in their appreciative interviews that the process of recognizing elements of success, positive experiences, and connections with others begins. As Witherell and Noddings (1991) write,

> Stories and narrative, whether personal or fictional, provide meaning and belonging in our lives. They attach us to others and to our own histories by providing a tapestry rich with threads of time, place, character, and even advice on what we might do with our lives. (p. 1)

Throughout the ages, stories have been "vehicles for making sense of our experiences, but they also help practitioners to determine a course of action to influence others" (Abma, 2003, p. 223). Stories have the ability to transfer cognitive, social, and cultural knowledge in ways that can be understood by a variety of listeners. Within the context of Appreciative Inquiry, this "narrative-rich environment" creates data that provide the means for analyzing high points and successes from which to build more positive experiences in the future (Ludema et al., 2003, p. 210). And perhaps most important of all, when people tell stories that remind them of hope, joy, and excitement, they often feel safer, are more collaborative, and, ultimately, they become more engaged in the change process.

Also fundamental to the concept of AI is the notion of *inner dialogue.* As research in the fields of medicine and mental health has shown, the voice we hear in our minds is a strong determinant of what we ultimately say or do. This voice projects both positive and negative images, and the outcomes are often related to the image projected by the inner dialogue. Bushe (2000) suggests that the "inner dialogue is mainly carried through the stories people tell themselves and each other to justify their interpretation of events and decisions" (p. 104). He further asserts that to change the organization, one has to change the inner dialogue; changing the inner dialogue then changes the stories and conversations people have with one another, and how people work together.

One influence on our inner dialogue comes from how we think about ourselves and what we know and how we learn—known as *metacognition* or "thinking about thinking." Metacognition refers to one's own thoughts about what we know or don't know and regulating how we go about learning (Huitt, 1997; Livingston, 1997). It is about people's awareness and abilities to predict their performances on various tasks and to have insight into how one thinks. For example, metacognition includes asking ourselves questions such as the following: What do I know about this subject, topic, or issue? Do I know what I need to know? Did I understand what I just heard, read, or saw? Do I know where I can get some information, knowledge? (Huitt, 1997). According to Cooperrider (1999), the relationship between metacognition and Appreciative Inquiry lies in the question, "is it possible to develop our own metacognitive capacity and thereby choose between positive and negative ways of construing the world?" (p.113). Citing examples from the world of sports, Cooperrider asserts,

> The best athletes are as successful as they are because of a highly developed metacognitive capacity of differential self-monitoring . . . this involves being able to systematically observe and analyze successful performances (positive self-monitoring) or unsuccessful performances (negative self-monitoring) and to be able to choose between the two cognitive processes when desired. (p. 113)

The implication for organizations and communities is that if we can learn about how we think, question how we come to know, and ultimately choose images of a positive future, then we will be able to realize the future we want.

Theories of *motivation* are also critical to understanding how and why Appreciative Inquiry works. Research conducted over the last 20 years has found that people will have more intrinsic motivation to act and change when they focus on past successes and use positive images to create a desired future. In particular, studies have shown that "intrinsic motivation is positive, internalized, self-owned, high-quality motivation that promotes higher quality learning, better task performance, reduced stress and tension, more productive adaptive approach to challenge, and increased relatedness to others" (Hardre, 2003, p. 61). On the other hand, "extrinsic motivation is externalized, other-caused, low quality motivation that does not consistently facilitate those valued outcomes" (p. 62). If this is true, then Appreciative Inquiry stimulates individuals' intrinsic motivation because they are able to focus on their own positive experiences and work toward creating more of them.

As discussed in this section, Appreciative Inquiry is grounded in several different theories and research studies. While AI principles and practices are drawn from a variety of disciplines, together they suggest that when people ask affirmative questions, reflect on and share past successful experiences, and use strengths-based language, they will have more energy, hope, and excitement about creating their desired future.

## Appreciative Inquiry Models

Cooperrider and several of his colleagues developed the 4-D model to describe each phase of the AI process. The four phases are *Discovery, Dream, Design,* and *Destiny*[1] (Cooperrider et al., 2003). Based on their own experiences and feedback received from clients, some AI practitioners have chosen to use a different set of labels that they believe are more accessible and/or descriptive of the four Appreciative Inquiry phases. The labels selected and used throughout this book are from the EnCompass model (see Figure 1.2). They are *Inquire, Imagine, Innovate,* and *Implement.*

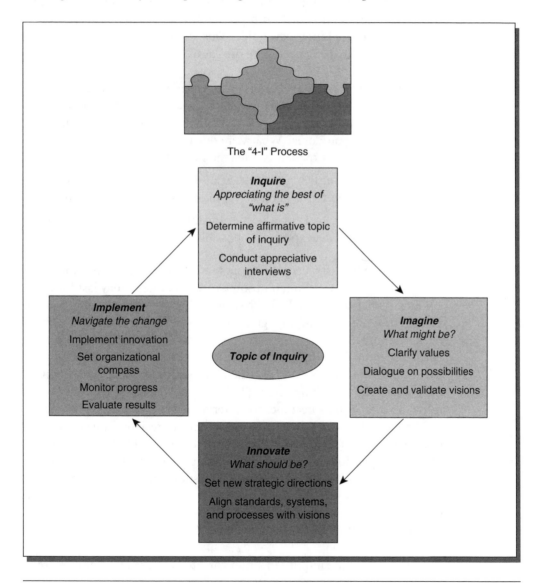

**Figure 1.2**    The EnCompass Model of Appreciative Inquiry

Source: Encompass LLC, Potomac, MD. Reprinted with permission.

What follows is a description of each of the four Appreciative Inquiry phases. It is important to note, however, that one of the benefits of AI is that it can easily be adapted to a particular culture, context, and environment. The choice of topic, the content of the questions, and how many of the phases are implemented all depend on the particularities of the organization and the purpose of the inquiry.

### Phase 1: Inquire—Appreciative Interviews

To begin the process, participants are asked to get into pairs, preferably with someone they interact with the least, and to interview each other based on a prepared interview guide. This guide typically includes a variation of the following generic core questions:

- *Peak Experience:* Think back on your experience with the XX program, and remember a time when you felt most energized and most proud to be part of this program. Tell a story about that time. What happened? What were you doing? What were others doing? What contributed to the success you experienced? Tell the story giving some detail.

- *Values:* Without being modest, what do you value most about yourself? . . . About this program? . . . About the work you do in this field?

- *Wishes:* If you had three wishes for this program to make more of these exceptional experiences possible, what would they be?

The facilitator instructs participants to interview each other for about 10–20 minutes each, although in some cases interviews may last for up to 2 hours. Participants are asked to pay close attention when listening and to assume they are listening to a great story, to help their interview partner recount more details of the story being told, and to listen for their partner's enthusiasm in telling that story. Under no circumstances are participant-listeners to interrupt the story with comments or a story of their own. After the allotted time, the facilitator signals the dyads to switch roles; the listener now becomes the interviewee and tells his or her story.

There may be times when variations to the appreciative interview questions need to be made. For example, if there is not enough time to use all of the core questions, a shorter version can be developed that might mean eliminating some or all of the *values* questions. Or, if there are special issues that need to be addressed by the inquiry, stories might be solicited on more than one topic.

The paired interviews allow for several things to occur:

- They begin the inquiry in a non-threatening, engaging, and interesting way.

- They help participants listen to the other person's story of success as defined by that person's values.

- They help participants get to know one another better.
- They serve as the foundation for determining the future success of the program.

If paired interviews are not possible, then individuals may tell their stories to the whole group. (See Chapter 4 for more information on various ways of conducting appreciative interviews.)

As indicated earlier, the core questions can be modified and adapted based on the participants' characteristics, the focus of the inquiry, and the time available. The following are sample alternative questions that could be used in this phase of the inquiry:

- As you reflect on your experience with the program, tell me a story about a highpoint.
- At what point in time did you feel most alive?
- When did you know it was working? How did you know it?
- When did you feel most successful in terms of your contributions to the project?
- Thinking about your department's contribution to the mission of the organization, what have you done to make the biggest difference?
- What are the most outstanding moments/stories from this organization's past that make you most proud to be a member of this organization?
- What are the things that give life to the organization when it is most alive, most effective, most in tune with the over-arching vision?
- What are we doing that should be preserved as we make changes?
- What were major milestones along the way?
- What kept you going and what was nurturing to you?
- Were there times when you said to yourself, "this is working, this is working!" What was happening during those times?
- If you could have waved a magic wand, and the project would have turned out exactly as you had planned, what would it have looked like?
- Describe a time when someone went out of his or her way to do something for you. What made it possible?
- If you could transform the ways in which you do your work, what would it look like and what would it take to happen?

It is important to understand that the telling of stories is not just to make people feel good and warm about themselves and each other. The power of the stories is in their ability to remind us of what success looked like and felt like—to relive the event and the feelings it generated; to remember that we can be successful, things can work, and that we have the capacity to bring life and energy to our work. They reinforce the notion that as co-contributors to the organization's goals, we often have more in common than we think. Most importantly, stories are useful data about dynamic moments of excellence that will provide the foundation for further analysis.

### Sharing Stories, Values, and Wishes

Following the paired interviews, participants share their stories in groups of six to eight, unless the group is too small. If this is the case, stories are shared with the large group. Notably, participants do not share their own story; rather, they tell their interview partner's story. Listening to one's story told by someone else celebrates the participant's experience and deepens one's own understanding of the experience as it is listened to while told by someone else. Participants are instructed to listen for themes as they hear the group's stories. If there is time, it is preferable that each small group might share some of the stories told at its table with the whole group. This would depend on the size of the group and the time available. The stories shared contain important information for the inquiry. Specifically, they

- Include information regarding how success is defined relevant to the topic being discussed.

- Provide information about how stakeholders have experienced the program.

- Articulate how the organization's systems operate in reality and not in the manuals.

- Illuminate the culture of the program and/or organization.

- Provide stakeholders a chance to reflect on and co-construct a larger story of the program and the organization.

- Allow shared realities to emerge, while also inviting isolated experiences and perspectives to be articulated and preserved.

The sharing of stories is a prerequisite for beginning the organization's reflection regarding its successes and strengths. It launches the inquiry with a celebration and the emergence of a vision of what the program or organization looks like when at its best. According to Liebler (1997), "The process of doing the appreciative interviews is as important as the data collected, for it is through the doing that the internal conversations within organizations are changed" (p. 33).

Once participants have told their stories, they are asked to describe the themes that emerged from their stories. If the group is large, participants might do this in small groups and record and report out their top five themes. Asking participants to derive themes from their stories is a means for initiating group reflection. These themes might be seen as "causes of success" that will be used throughout the next phases of the inquiry.

After participants reflect on the themes from the stories, they share the *values* and *wishes* that came from the interviews. As participants share the values, two things tend to happen: (1) they identify shared values and appreciate others' ideas about how to fulfill those values in the workplace; and (2) they are exposed to others' values that may not be a priority for them and see what others need if they are to excel. Sharing values makes explicit the fundamental motivation of those who are part of a program or organization. It also clarifies the standards people use to judge their experiences—the way they understand purpose, performance, and impact. These values are fundamental to the later phases of the inquiry process.

Participants' responses to the *wishes* question may later become translated into recommendations, as they tend to reflect participants' intimate knowledge of the program or organization. Participants' wishes also reveal their beliefs regarding

- Aspects of the program or organization that need improvement
- Aspects of the program or organization that stakeholders would like explored with more attention
- The potential benefits of the inquiry process

In many ways, the appreciative interviews are the heart and soul of the AI process. Consequently, they contribute to the inquiry's success in a number of ways:

- They ground participants' "success" in a real experience as opposed to an opinion of what is positive in the program.
- They require that "success" be a personal experience, thus making the participant both excited to tell it and directly knowledgeable about it.
- They make the values of the storyteller explicit, giving internal consistency and alignment of the subjective criteria based on which the storyteller considers this story a success.
- They require participants to reflect on the causes and contributing factors for that "success" highlighting systemic and unusual factors, and personal strengths leading to that success. This enables participants to begin thinking more positively about what needs to be present to ensure "success" for the subject of the inquiry. For example, participants may begin to wonder: Are there some elements that are always present, but are not integrated consistently in the project? Are there elements that are unusual or were present by chance, but might be built in?
- They generate recommendations from the three *wishes* question that flow from the analysis of the successful experience and will later be used to develop future actions.

## Phase 2: Imagine

The next step in the Appreciative Inquiry process is developing a vision for the future of the program or organization. Participants are first invited to reflect individually on a question such as the following:

> *Imagine that it is 2–3 years from now and you are preparing for an awards ceremony to celebrate the program's excellence.* The New York Times *wishes to write an article on this exceptional program. You are so proud to be part of this program. What is happening to make you proud? What are people saying? What is happening internally in the program or organization? What changes and/or events made this success possible?*

In the instructions, participants are encouraged to be bold but realistic and to stretch their imaginations. After quiet reflection, individuals or small groups (or all together if the group is small) develop visions of a successful future of the program or organization. After the visions are developed individually and in small groups, they are shared and discussed with the large group. Groups may also be invited to draw pictures of their visions. These images are particularly effective at tapping into an individual's or group's creative energy. And, for some, drawing images may be more effective than words in conveying an idea or concept. This visioning exercise helps participants think about what they need to help them construct a positive future, and prepares them for implementing the results of the inquiry. It is important to select a point in the future that is far enough away that people are able to be daring but close enough so that they can see it as a future that builds directly on the actions of the present. In general, two to three years is a reasonable target; however, one can vary that number depending on the particular circumstances of the inquiry and participants' cultural perceptions of time.

## Phase 3: Innovate

It is during the *Innovate* phase of AI that participants' past successes and visions for the future become concrete actionable possibilities—it is when participants recognize how change can occur and what needs to happen to make it a reality. The *Innovate* phase begins by having participants identify one of the themes that emerged from their interviews and visions. Participants can work on more than one theme, but it is useful if they work on one theme at a time. Once they have selected a theme, they are asked to develop *provocative propositions* (also called design statements, opportunity, or possibility statements). These statements, which are always written in the present tense and are affirmative, are intended to bridge the best of "what is" with participants' visions of "what might be." They should stretch the imagination, go beyond the obvious, and ultimately represent elements of the organization's social architecture. The social architecture represents those things in an organization that are needed to support the implementation of the future desired state. Cooperrider et al. (2003, p. 144) suggest that the following be considered and represented in participants' provocative propositions:

- Business processes
- Communication systems
- Culture
- Customer relations
- Education and training
- Leadership
- Management practices
- Policies
- Shared values
- Social responsibility
- Strategy
- Structure
- Systems
- Technology
- Beliefs about power and authority
- Relationships
- Staff/people
- Governance structure
- Knowledge management system
- Practices and principles

Guidelines for developing effective propositions can be seen in Figure 1.3.

- Is it *provocative?* Does it stretch, challenge, or interrupt the status quo?
- Is it *grounded?* Are examples available that illustrate the ideal as a real possibility? Is it grounded in the organization's collective history?
- Is it *desired?* Do you want it as a preferred future?
- Is it stated in *affirmative* and *bold* terms?
- Does it follow a *social architecture* approach?
- Does it expand the "*zone of proximal development*"?
- Is it a *participative* process?
- Is it used to stimulate *intergenerational learning?*
- Is there balanced management of *continuity, novelty, and transition?*

**Figure 1.3**    Guidelines for Developing Effective Provocative Propositions
Source: Cooperrider et al., 2003, p. 148.

The *Innovate* phase is reportedly the most difficult part of the AI process. It is the time when participants get to work making visions concrete, deciding on how to shape their systems and relationships differently to move toward their vision. Action planning is hard work, regardless of what methodology is being used. It becomes easier, however, when the issues are fairly straightforward, and when participants are ready to move forward. Then, provocative propositions can be written with less difficulty and within a shorter time period of one or more meetings. In other cases, the *Innovate* phase may need to stretch over a period of weeks or months in order to gather more information and consult with others. For example, the *Innovate* phase of an Appreciative Inquiry on affordable housing in Dubuque, Iowa, took 1 year and two summit meetings of a representative stakeholders group, with the period in between summit meetings devoted to interviews of community participants, and researching key regulatory issues (Webb, 2000).

The following are examples of provocative propositions. Depending on the amount of time available and the topic of the inquiry, provocative propositions can be written as paragraphs or simple sentences.

## Inquiry Topic: Community/ Neighborhood Development

- While all of our city's neighborhoods are attractive, livable, well-maintained areas that accommodate the varied social, economic, and cultural groups that make up our community, our older neighborhoods are a unique economic and aesthetic asset preserved with particular vigilance by all. Regardless of location, neighborhoods are clean, well-lit, accessible, and safe, with adequate green space and other appropriate amenities.

- Constant attention to neighborhood health and development has resulted in a broad range of housing options ranging from subsidized and low-cost to the highest level of market value.

- Our community has an occupancy rate of 95% and provides opportunities for rental, owner occupied, transitional, special needs, and investor opportunities in housing development.

- Realizing that buildings and the infrastructure are only part of neighborhood development, our community has made *people issues* a priority. Cooperation and collaboration are invited and encouraged with and between neighborhood associations, human service agencies, city departments and commissions, churches, schools, families, and other organizations.

## Inquiry Topic: Experiencing Passion in Our Work

*Quality of Work Life*

- We conduct an annual evaluation of the work environment.
- The workspace is physically designed to encourage communication and community.
- There are different kinds of opportunities for employees to socialize.
- Employees vote on how best to spend a portion of the budget (non-program) in ways that have a positive impact on the quality of employee life.
- The organization's leadership models and supports family/workplace balance; we offer child care in multiple sites and offer flexible work schedules.

*Employee Recognition*

- We have monthly lunches where individuals and teams are recognized for their contributions to the organization.
- There is a bulletin board announcing employee news and accomplishments.
- We have a regular e-journal that highlights employees' contributions, success stories, and program impacts.

*Communication*

- We maintain a Web-based clearinghouse of resources that includes best practices and lessons learned from various projects.
- Communication is clear, uses appropriate channels, and reflects the voices of customers and staff.
- We seek ongoing feedback from our internal and external customers.
- We look for opportunities to bring various internal customers together to talk about how we're doing.

## Inquiry Topic: Customer Satisfaction

- Our customers speak highly of our organization and recommend it to others. Seventy-five percent of our organization's revenues come from repeat purchasers. Account managers work hard to develop personal relationships with each customer. We have a highly automated contact management database, which has three components:
  - Intelligent outbound identification and calling
  - Personalized Web transaction system customized to historical buying patterns

- Highly targeted electronic marketing focused on buying patterns and vertical markets
- Our company name is a household name and our Internet address is bookmarked on every possible purchaser's computer.

As indicated earlier, participants often find the *Innovate* phase to be somewhat challenging. In part this is due to the amount of conceptual effort it takes to translate their successful experiences and visions into clear and specific actions they would like the organization to take as part of the change effort. This process may also require a reciprocal, negotiated dialogue with large numbers of people about how they will get organized and what changes they will make to accomplish their vision. To assist participants in developing the provocative propositions, various group facilitation and design processes can be employed. For example, the facilitator might use the concept of the *Deep Dive*, which is a design process that promotes creativity and innovation by bringing together people with many different types of expertise and organizes them in an intensive collaboration that delves deeply into different areas of their design goal (Kelley & Littman, 2001). During this process participants may engage in brainstorming, discussions, additional research, or field visits; conduct interviews; administer surveys; or develop models and prototypes.

Another strategy would be to use De Bono's (1985) *Six Thinking Hats* activity. This exercise is used to help groups experience several different kinds of thinking perspectives, such as considering information needs, bringing passion, caution and problem prevention, creativity and new ideas, alignment of definition, purpose and stocktaking, and values and appreciation. While there are many variations for using the Six Hats activity, one approach is to distribute hats to all participants with some possibly having the same hat depending on the group size, and the topic of discussion. The task is for participants to express their opinions on the topic quickly from their hat's perspective. Then, the hats are exchanged, and the process is repeated for a new topic. A benefit of this exercise is that it invites a wider diversity of considerations in planning and decision making, in ways that result in deeper and more informed thinking.

Process mapping through the development of *flow charts* is another tool that can be applied in the *Innovate* phase. A flow chart helps clarify how things are currently working and how they could be changed to move closer to the theme of the Appreciative Inquiry. Developing a flow chart helps to create a common understanding about the process under review (Franco, Newman, Murphy, & Mariani, 1997).

Using Open Space technology is another way to engage participants in this phase. For example, Odell (2005, personal communication) explains that he asks each person to take a piece of paper and to create a "short, sweet advertisement with a picture, logo, and/or a few choice words" that will be used to "sell" their vision. Participants take turns "selling their ad," in an attempt to recruit others to join their effort. They then post these on the wall and collectively work out the clustering of ads where there are similar ideas or missions. These clusters become "dream teams" that go on through the next and final phase of the AI process.

## Phase 4: Implement

This phase of the AI process represents taking action on the provocative propositions. When participants are ready to self-organize, they choose a topic based on their individual motivations, passions, and interests. They then publicly declare their intended actions to carry out the implementation of the provocative propositions (Cooperrider & Whitney, 1999). Participants usually select one or more of the themes identified during the inquiry and meet with others who have similar interests. As they reflect on and discuss the work that has been done on their chosen issue or topic, they make plans for how they can make the propositions become a reality. It should be noted that there may be times when the facilitator may need to help participants negotiate and mediate which, how, when, and where the provocative propositions will be implemented. Processes such as Future Search and Open Space are particularly useful when there are competing resources, limited time, and different ideas about what is important and what changes should be made. Implementing the provocative propositions may at times be simple and quick, but in others, efforts may last for months, depending on the complexity of the tasks. When the formal Appreciative Inquiry process has been completed, participants often "walk away with a sense of commitment, confidence and affirmation that they have been successful. They also know clearly how to make more moments of success" (Hammond, 1996, p. 7). More importantly, they continue to have different kinds of conversations and continue to use the Appreciative Inquiry language to do their work.

Describing this as the final phase of the AI process is rather misleading since, in fact, most proponents of Appreciative Inquiry suggest that it is critical to "keep the conversation going" even after an inquiry has been completed (Whitney, 2002, personal communication). However, the *Implement* phase invites participants to celebrate and act on the work they have accomplished through their engagement in the *Inquire, Imagine,* and *Innovate* phases. Whitney and Trosten-Bloom (2003) suggest that participants address the following questions:

- *How will we learn about the gains we've already made?* Surveys? Appreciative Inquiry? Open storytelling sessions?
- *How will we celebrate?* What needs to happen to keep people aware of and excited about ongoing innovations? How might recognition inspire ongoing action?

- *What are our parameters for self-organized action?* Time? Resources? Domains?
- *How shall we self-organize?* Should we engage existing work groups, or form separate AI Learning Teams?
- *How will we support success?* What resources, support, and expertise do people need? Who are the best people to provide what's needed? (p. 218, emphasis in the original)

To help participants answer these questions, Whitney and Trosten-Bloom offer the following steps for implementing this phase (p. 219):

- Review, communicate, and celebrate accomplishments
- Generate a list of potential actions
- Self-organize for inspired action projects
- Support success of self-organized projects
- Systemic application of Appreciative Inquiry

It should be noted that as various actions are taken to implement the group's provocative propositions, additional Appreciative Inquiries should be initiated to monitor the effectiveness and success of these initiatives.

## Appreciative Inquiry and "Problems"

When people first learn about Appreciative Inquiry, they often question what happens to the *problems*. A common first reaction is that AI's focus on success means that the problems, issues, or challenges are ignored or even denied. However, this is fundamentally incorrect. Appreciative Inquiry does in fact address issues, challenges, problems, and conflict, but it does so by shifting the focus and language from one of deficits to one of hope and possibilities based on what has worked in the past. This reframing means that the spirit of the inquiry is not about "fault finding, harsh judgment, or culpability, but rather in the exploration of what *might be* if changes were made" (Elliott, 1999, p. 51; emphasis in the original). As Banaga (1998) further explains,

Appreciative Inquiry does not turn a blind eye on "negative" situations or "deficit-oriented" realities in organizations; it does not substitute a "rosy" and "romantic" picture for an "objective" and "realistic" one. It accepts these realities for what they are—areas in need of conversations and transformation. . . . But AI intentionally shifts the focus of the inquiry and intervention to those realities that are sources of vitality. (p. 263)

Whitney and Trosten-Bloom (2003) add, "We do not dismiss accounts of conflict, problems, or stress. We simply do not use them as the basis of analysis or action" (p. 18). And, as Elliott (1999) reminds us, "it is deliberately called the appreciative approach, not the affirmative approach or the positive approach or the uncritical approach" (p. 10). What these writers suggest, then, is that problems do get addressed during an AI process, but not through traditional problem-solving approaches. Rather, Appreciative Inquiry solves problems by focusing on what to do more of based on what has worked, which translates into knowing what to do less of that has not worked.

Given how endemic problem-solving approaches are in organizations, and how difficult it is for some to believe that AI does not ignore problems, it is worth considering the underlying assumptions of problem-solving approaches when addressing organizational challenges and issues. According to Watkins and Mohr (2001, p. 196), these assumptions include

- There is some ideal way for things to be.
- If a situation is not as we would like it to be, it is a "problem" to be solved.
- The way to solve a problem is to break it into parts and analyze it.
- If we find a broken part and fix it, the whole will be fixed.

And, most problem-solving approaches involve

- Identifying what is wrong
- Analyzing the causes
- Deciding on goals to fix these causes
- Making a plan that will achieve the goals
- Implementing the plan
- Evaluating whether or not we fixed the problem

While the problem-solving approach may be effective in some contexts for particular kinds of problems, it is by no means the best or only way to address many of the critical issues facing today's organizations. Cooperrider (quoted in Zemke, 1999) suggests that the problem-solving approach is painfully slow, asks people to look backward at yesterday's failures and their causes, and rarely results in a new vision. He further asserts, "Problem-solving approaches are notorious for placing blame and generating defensiveness. They sap your energy and tax your mind, and don't advance the organization's evolution beyond a slow crawl" (p. 28). Reframing the problem-solving process using Appreciative Inquiry means (Watkins & Mohr, 2001, pp. 196–197)

- Looking at our experience in the area that we want to improve in order to discover the times when things were going well—times when we felt excited, successful, joyful

- Collectively creating from these stories a description for what we want (our image of the ideal)
- Asking others how they have successfully dealt with a similar situation
- Sharing our images, discovering the images that others hold, and continually re-creating a generative and creative future throughout the system

When comparing these two approaches, two critical differences emerge: (1) the language used—deficit-based vs. affirmative, and (2) the fact that some problem-solving approaches do not take into account the whole system—parts vs. holistic. Some writers suggest that as people talk about problems using deficit-based language, the problem itself will grow in magnitude and detail and participants' energy and hope will be exhausted. And when people fail to consider the whole system and only look at the parts, they will often draw the wrong conclusion about what's going on and make decisions that do not solve the problem. Anderson, Gergen, McNamee, Cooperrider, Gergen, and Whitney (2001) suggest that "as the problem gains in dimension and implication, so can it seem more burdensome and intractable. Energies are drained, and the group meeting becomes a chore" (p. 31). While these authors do not advocate avoiding the discussion of problems, they recommend replacing problem talk with possibility talk. They argue that problems do not energize people, but, rather, it is their visions of possibilities, something valued or desired that motivates people to act. Barrett (1995) further suggests that an analytic problem-solving approach has serious limitations that include: (a) it is inherently conservative, (b) it furthers a deficiency orientation, (c) it furthers a fragmented view of the world, and (d) it results in further separation between stakeholders (pp. 37–39). Finally, focusing on problems has the tendency to oppress rather than encourage asking questions and it often leads to reinforcing defensive routines (see Hammond & Mayfield, 2004, for an excellent discussion on the topic undiscussables and what happens when people are afraid or uncertain about asking questions and engaging in constructive dialogue).

We do not believe Appreciative Inquiry should be thought of as a wholesale replacement of problem-solving or gap analysis techniques. Certain problem-solving approaches may need to be applied in specific contexts. As Hammond (in Zemke, 1999) explains,

> If you are in an airplane with a sputtering engine or you are having a heart attack, you have a problem in need of solving. You don't want someone asking appreciative-inquiry-type questions just then. You want fault-finding and fault-analysis and fault-fixing. (p. 32)

We would add, however, that the origin of the problem and how to avoid it in the future might be best explored through an AI approach!

# Applications of Appreciative Inquiry in Organization Development

To illustrate how Appreciative Inquiry has been used for organizational development and change purposes, two examples that demonstrate AI's flexibility and adaptability are provided in this book. The first example, presented in this chapter, describes a one-day Appreciative Inquiry that was conducted to increase the collaboration between two programs at the Centers for Disease Control and Prevention in Atlanta, Georgia. The second case example, which is full of rich details, is located in the appendix to this book. This case describes a whole-systems change process that involved the transformation of Evergreen Cove, a nonprofit organization that provides alternative health care to a rural community in Maryland. This transformation was accomplished over more than a year, and has spurred grassroots action, member activism making the center more accessible to those in need, and new alliances that have established funding sources that may not have been available to Evergreen Cove prior to the AI change process.

---

**Case Study 1**

## Developing Successful Collaborations at the Centers for Disease Control and Prevention (CDC)[2]

An outside evaluator recommended that collaboration be improved between two programs at the Centers for Disease Control and Prevention (CDC) that provide services to the same client population: the WISEWOMAN (**W**ell-**I**ntegrated **S**creening and **E**valuation for **Wom**en **A**cross the **N**ation) program and the National Breast and Cervical Cancer Early Detection Program (NBCCEDP). Both programs serve low-income women, with WISEWOMAN screening for blood pressure and cholesterol and the NBCCEDP program providing free or discounted breast and cervical cancer screening, and follow-up and treatment. Both programs shared the goal of making services more convenient for women by providing multiple screening tests during the same health care appointment ("one stop shopping"). However, the CDC WISEWOMAN and NBCCEDP staff personally identified with one program or the other and focused on the health services provided by their own program rather than on *all* of the services available during the health care appointment. CDC WISEWOMAN and NBCCEDP staff resided in completely different organizational groups, worked in buildings about a half-mile apart, and functioned separately. Staff from the two programs indicated that they wanted health care delivery sites to coordinate services for women and hoped that collaboration would increase the efficiency of sites. Ironically, however the outside evaluator noted that some CDC staff felt that their own attempts at collaboration at CDC seemed to drain away both their time and energy needed to accomplish their work.

*(Continued)*

(Continued)

In response to the finding of the external evaluator, a NBCCEDP staff member was assigned as a liaison to help improve the way in which the two programs collaborate. Rather than viewing the need to improve collaboration as a problem, the liaison decided to take a more appreciative approach to find ways for increasing collaboration. With the help of an Appreciative Inquiry workshop facilitator, staff from WISEWOMAN and NBCCEDP were invited to participate in a one-day Appreciative Inquiry workshop on the topic of "Successful Collaboration." Participants were told that during the day they would be identifying ways in which they could strengthen their collaborative efforts between the two programs.

All four phases of Appreciative Inquiry were used during the workshop. For the first phase, *Inquire,* participants were provided the following information:

> Organizations at their best encourage exceptional partnerships and collaborations in which all parties have an equal voice and share a responsibility for creating communities and organizations of the future. Such collaborations require honesty, trust, respect, open communication, enthusiasm, and a common interest as well as the ability to agree to disagree.

Participants were then asked to form pairs and to interview each other for 10 minutes (each) using the following questions:

1. Best Experience: Reflect for a moment and remember a time when you were collaborating with others to accomplish a goal or task, and it was exciting, effective, productive, even fun! Describe this experience and the qualities that made it so satisfying and successful.
   - What was it about this collaboration that made it a peak experience?
   - What were the conditions that allowed this collaboration to be so productive?
   - What did you do to make it so successful? What did others do?
   - What do you think was the root cause of this effective collaboration?

2. Values: What do you value most about
   - Yourself, and
   - The ways you approach collaborating with others?

3. Three Wishes: If you had three wishes that would ensure more successful collaborations in your work setting, what would they be?

Participants interviewed each other, presented each other's stories to two other pairs (small groups of six), and identified and wrote the themes from their stories on a flip-chart page.

In the second phase, *Imagine,* participants were asked to stay in their groups of six and to consider and respond to the following hypothetical situation:

> Imagine that you have been asleep for 5 years and it is now 2009. As you awake, you look around and see that the NBCCEDP and WISEWOMAN program staff are the model of effective collaboration. Not only have they created strategies, tools, and systems for collaborating, but they also approach the

majority of tasks and challenges in a collaborative way. Collaboration has become the way work gets done.

Imagine that the two programs have been so successful in their collaboration efforts that they have received a congressional award for their efforts. Two weeks after receiving "The National Congressional Bipartisan Award for Excellence in Collaboration in Government" at a Washington ceremony, imagine that you receive a phone call from the producers of the *Today* show, who want you and your colleagues to appear on next Thursday's show. With the award in hand, you arrive in New York and are escorted to the set.

Imagine that Matt Lauer begins the interview by asking you to describe what collaboration looks like and how it works. He further asks: How does collaboration happen? How do you sustain collaboration? What do people do when they collaborate? What does collaboration feel like? What is happening?

What does your team tell Matt Lauer?

Participants were also instructed to draw an image representing their idea of collaboration.

After each group shared the themes from their hypothetical interview with Matt Lauer from the *Imagine* phase and their visual representations, they then moved into the *Innovate* phase. Staying in their groups of six, they were asked to review the themes that emerged from their group's discussions during the *Inquire* and *Imagine* interviews and discussions. Then, drawing on their insights from developing these themes, the participants were asked to create 3–5 provocative propositions. These were to be written in the affirmative and present tense, describing how the two programs "are developing and sustaining successful collaborations." Participants were instructed that provocative propositions should reflect various organizational elements such as leadership, strategy, structures, systems, communication, management practices, internal customer relations, culture, people, values, competencies, roles and responsibilities, or work processes. Participants wrote their group's provocative propositions on sticky notes and placed the notes on multiple pieces of flip-chart paper that were positioned along the room's wall. They were then asked to post their propositions next to those from other groups that seemed to be similar in focus.

The final phase, *Implement,* is where participants have the opportunity to act on the ideas that they generated in the provocative propositions. Again, participants were asked to stay in their small groups and to

- Discuss the different provocative propositions.
- Identify one or two provocative propositions that appeal to you and that you might like to work on—either as an individual or as a group.
- Develop two or three action items you will commit to making happen in the next 6 months.

The workshop ended with each group reporting to the larger group what they were planning to do to implement the provocative propositions.

After the Appreciative Inquiry workshop, a majority of participants reported on a written evaluation of the workshop that they felt more confident that they could collaborate successfully with staff from the other program. Many indicated that they were

*(Continued)*

┌─ (Continued) ─────────────────────────────────────────┐

planning to use Appreciative Inquiry in their work and/or with their families and religious groups. Positive feelings about the appreciative process were reflected in the following comments: "This was easier than I expected and not threatening." "Nice to work as a group together. Sets a good precedent," and, "We've made the first step!"

Symbolically, conducting a joint workshop with the two programs was the first effort toward greater collaboration. During the provocative proposition phase (*Innovate*), staff from both programs spontaneously formed a group that promised to meet at least monthly to exchange information on the programs' activities. As a result of the AI workshop, this group has been meeting for over a year and is finding additional ways to work together. For example, staff have attended the annual meeting of each other's program, and the managers of the two programs have initiated periodic meetings. In addition, program documents are now on a common computer network drive so that staff from both programs can share references and access information easily. Finally, having project officers from each program travel together to conduct joint site visits in places where both NBCCEDP and WISEWOMAN services are provided in the field has enhanced collaboration.

Government programs are often the subjects of external review. In this case, an external evaluator recommended that the two programs "must continue working to improve collaboration and create a more integrated approach." By using the Appreciative Inquiry approach, the workshop experience built on the prior successes and existing skills of staff members as a means for improving collaboration.

└───────────────────────────────────────────────────────┘

┌───────────────────────────────────────────────────────┐
│ **Case Study 2**

### Using Appreciative Inquiry at Evergreen Cove Holistic Health Center (Full Text Presented in the Appendix)[3]

This case study is an example of a full AI change process that was implemented over a period of almost two years. It is an excellent example of how deep and messy and creative and engaging AI can be, and it also shows how masterful the facilitator needs to be when taking on such a large-scale change process. This case study can help the reader appreciate that Appreciative Inquiry is not just about "technique," it is also about a different and exciting way of seeing the world, embracing change, and seeking life-giving new direction for people and organizations. Because of its length, this case study is presented in the appendix of this book.

└───────────────────────────────────────────────────────┘

## Summary

This chapter provided a historical and theoretical overview of Appreciative Inquiry and its application to organizational development and change. It has emphasized the need for organizations and communities to focus on their assets and strengths versus their problems as a means for creating a better future. Organizations that embrace AI as an approach for change make a deliberate choice about discovering their path to change through an appreciation and exploration of their peak moments of success. The organization's members engage in very different kinds of conversations that enhance their sense of connection to their work, their colleagues, and the organization. Through storytelling, they increase their confidence to think and act creatively and to seek change that brings satisfaction, hope, and joy to their work. As a result, the organization becomes more open to becoming a "learning organization" that is better able to respond to continuous internal and external changes more quickly and successfully.

# Notes

1.  The fourth phase in Cooperrider's original work was called *Delivery*. It was changed to *Destiny* because he felt it did not go far enough in communicating the liberating impact of AI work (Cooperrider & Whitney, 2000, p. 15).

2.  Contributed by Patricia Poindexter and Diane Dunet, CDC, National Center for Chronic Disease Prevention and Health Promotion (NCCDPHP), Division of Nutrition and Physical Activity (DNPA), Chronic Disease Nutrition Branch.

3.  Implemented by EnCompass LLC, Potomac, MD.

# Using Appreciative Inquiry in Evaluation Practice 2

*When you change the way you look at things, the things you look at change.*

—Dr. Wayne Dyer

This chapter builds on what we know about Appreciative Inquiry by suggesting that it offers evaluators an exciting and effective approach for designing and implementing evaluation studies. Recognizing that not all readers may be familiar with evaluation's history as a discipline, this chapter first highlights selected milestones that mark the development of the evaluation profession. Then, it describes selected evaluation approaches and methods that are most relevant to understanding the ways in which AI can be used for evaluation purposes. Following this discussion, it addresses how the evaluator's role is constantly evolving based on the dynamic nature of organizations and the communities in which they work. For those who wish to learn more about the history of evaluation and additional evaluation theories and methods, there are many fine books that provide a comprehensive treatment of these topics (e.g., Alkin, 2004; Fitzpatrick, Sanders, & Worthen, 2003; Patton, 1997; Posavac & Carey, 2003; Rossi, Lipsey, & Freeman, 2004; Russ-Eft & Preskill, 2001).

Similarities between evaluation and Appreciative Inquiry are discussed in the next section of this chapter. Although evaluation and AI are situated in different disciplines and thus have different origins and practices, they share several similarities with regard to program and organization improvement and to informed and confident decision making. In particular, Appreciative Inquiry has much in common with participatory, collaborative, and learning approaches to evaluation. To illustrate how AI has been applied within evaluation contexts, brief summaries of several evaluation studies are presented. The chapter concludes with an introduction to three particular applications of Appreciative Inquiry to evaluation, which are further explored and illustrated in Chapters 3–5.

## Modern-Day Evaluation

From the early 1900s through the 1950s, evaluation was primarily focused on educational testing and the development of mental and skill assessments for schools and the military. However, in the 1960s the landscape of evaluation theory and practice began to change when President Lyndon Johnson allocated millions of dollars to fight the War on Poverty and to create The Great Society. The result was a watershed of innovative programs to improve education, mental health, and the welfare system, and to reduce unemployment, crime, and urban deterioration. The 1965 Elementary and Secondary Education Act (ESEA) earmarked millions of dollars in grant money for the purpose of improving the education of disadvantaged students throughout the country (Fitzpatrick, Sanders, & Worthen, 2003; House, 1993; Russ-Eft & Preskill, 2001). To ensure that the federal monies would be used to benefit the children for whom it was intended, Senator Robert Kennedy worked to make certain that an amendment was attached to the ESEA bill that mandated local education agencies to submit evaluation plans and the state agencies to submit summary reports. These reports included a description of how the money was spent and the effectiveness of the program based on objective measures of student achievement that resulted from the money provided (Cronbach, 1980). As a result, the requirement to evaluate the program's effectiveness and impact became part of every federal grant (House, 1993; McLaughlin, 1975; Rossi, Lipsey, & Freeman, 2004). By 1978, approximately $140 million had been spent on evaluating federal social programs (Levitan & Wurzburg, 1979).

It is important to note that prior to the 1960s, there were no university courses or workshops on evaluation, and few individuals called themselves "program evaluators." Instead, those who conducted evaluations in the 1960s and early 1970s were typically university-based social science researchers and psychometricians. As House (1993) explains, "Prior to 1965, evaluation was a minor activity, a sideline engaged in academics as extra consulting work" (p. 15). Given that these individuals were often educated and trained in social science research methods, they were inclined to design and implement evaluations using experimental and quasi-experimental designs. They believed that utilizing quantitative outcome measures could "meet the demand for surrogate measures of economic growth" (House, 1993, p. 5), and that these approaches would not only illuminate the causes of social problems, but that the solutions and fixes to the problems could be easily clarified and implemented.

It soon became apparent that evaluation needed to be differentiated from research. One of the first to do so was Michael Scriven (1967, 1991) who declared that the role of the evaluator is to make value judgments. He views evaluation as

> a process of determining the merit, worth, or value of something, or the product of that process. Terms used to refer to this process or part of it include: appraise, analyze, assess, critique, examine, grade, inspect, judge, rate, rank review, study, test. . . . The evaluation process normally involves some identification of relevant standards of merit, worth, or value; some investigation of the performance of evaluands on these standards; and some integration or synthesis of the results to achieve an overall evaluation or set of associated evaluations. (Scriven, 1991, p. 139)

Scriven's view implies a summative function of evaluation. That is, evaluation is best used to answer questions such as the following: Is the program good? Is the program worth the costs? Does the program add value? The answers to these questions may lead to decisions concerning whether a program should be continued, or whether to expand or retract a program's services.

As legislators began to read copious evaluation reports, they came to believe that the evaluations were not only poorly conceived, designed, and administered, but also that the results were not very useful. Since the evaluations had focused on determining what worked and what didn't work and on making judgments of worth or value, there was little information about how the programs could improve. This dissatisfaction, and increasing opportunities for conducting evaluations, contributed to the development of new evaluation theories, models, and strategies in the 1970s. Some of these efforts led to establishing evaluation approaches that did not rely on quantitative experimental designs; instead, they called for the collection of qualitative data using naturalistic, ethnographic, case study designs. Also during this time, Michael Q. Patton wrote a book called *Utilization-Focused Evaluation* (1976, 1986, 1997) in which he emphasized the importance of designing and implementing evaluations in ways that maximize the use of their findings. He offers the following definition of evaluation:

> Program evaluation is the systematic collection of information about the activities, characteristics, and outcomes of programs to make judgments about the program, improve program effectiveness, and/or inform decisions about future programming. Utilization-focused program evaluation (as opposed to program evaluation in general) is evaluation done for and with specific, intended primary users for specific, intended uses. (1997, p. 23)

In comparison to Scriven's (1991) definition, Patton's view of evaluation places more emphasis on program improvement and the use of an evaluation's results.

As an increasing number of people became involved in evaluation, they sought ways in which they could come together and share their knowledge and experiences. The result was the establishment of two U.S.-based professional organizations in 1976—the Evaluation Network (mostly university professors and school-based evaluators) and the Evaluation Research Society (mostly government-based evaluators and some university evaluators). In 1985, these two organizations merged to form the American Evaluation Association (AEA, www.eval.org), which numbers more than 4,200 members worldwide (AEA, April 2005).

In spite of President Ronald Reagan's significant budget cuts and the elimination of the evaluation requirement in many federal grant programs, the evaluation profession continued to grow and evolve throughout the 1980s. It was a decade marked with intense debates over the most appropriate approaches to conducting evaluation—often referred to as the "Quantitative-Qualitative" divide. By the early 1990s, however, a truce was called. By then, most evaluators agreed that (a) an evaluation's design and data collection methods should be guided by the questions the evaluation seeks to address, and (b) most evaluations generally benefit from using a mixed-method approach (using quantitative and qualitative data collection methods); arguing whether quantitative designs and data are better than qualitative designs and data was divisive and not productive for the growing profession.

By the 1990s, evaluators grew increasingly interested in, and committed to, using participatory, collaborative, democratic, empowerment, and learning-oriented approaches to evaluation. According to Cousins (2003), participatory evaluation is

> An approach where persons trained in evaluation methods and logic work in collaboration with those not so trained to implement evaluation activities. That is, members of the evaluation community and members of other stakeholder groups relative to the evaluand each participate in some or all of the shaping and/or technical activities required to produce evaluation knowledge leading to judgments of merit and worth and support for program decision making. (p. 245)

Many evaluators believed that the involvement of stakeholders would not only increase their understanding of evaluation, and that it would better serve their information needs, but that it would also increase stakeholders' commitment to using the results.

At the same time, evaluators working in the U.S. government sector found themselves in a very different milieu. Calls for increased government program accountability within the United States resulted in the

Government Performance Results Act (GPRA). The law required that all U.S. federal agencies develop performance-monitoring systems. An emphasis on oversight and compliance meant that evaluators needed to develop systems and methods for collecting data to meet these new requirements.

By the end of the 1990s and into the early part of the 21st century, many evaluators were frequently using participatory and collaborative forms of evaluation. After years of working with stakeholders, some evaluators began to study what and how stakeholders were learning from their participation in evaluation studies (Cousins, 1999; Cousins, Goh, Clark, & Lee, 2004; Forss, Cracknell, & Samset, 1994; Forss, Rebein, & Carlsson, 2002; Owen & Lambert, 1995; Owen & Rogers, 1999; Patton, 1994, 1997; Preskill & Torres, 1999; Preskill, Zuckerman, & Matthews, 2003; Rossman & Rallis, 2000). These evaluators suggest that by being intentional about learning throughout the evaluation; by encouraging dialogue and reflection; questioning assumptions, values, and beliefs; and by creating learning spaces and opportunities, individuals may come to more fully understand the program being evaluated, the organization or community, themselves, each other, and, ultimately, evaluation practice. Interest in stakeholders' learning from evaluation has led some evaluators to propose that evaluative inquiry can be a catalyst for group and organizational learning as well as individual learning. From their perspective, Preskill and Torres (1999) suggest that evaluative inquiry is

> An ongoing process for investigating and understanding critical organization issues. It is an approach to learning that is fully integrated with an organization's work practices, and as such, it engenders (a) organization members' interest and ability in exploring critical issues using evaluation logic, (b) organization members' involvement in evaluative processes, and (c) the personal and professional growth of individuals within the organization. (pp. 1–2)

This definition emphasizes that evaluation can produce much more than a report of findings, and rather than being event-driven, evaluation should be ongoing and part of everyone's job. As a result, evaluative inquiry for learning focuses on (Preskill, 2005, p. 146)

- Program and organizational processes as well as outcomes
- Shared individual, team, and organizational learning
- Education and training of organizational practitioners in inquiry skills
- Collaboration, cooperation, and participation
- Establishing linkages between learning and performance
- Searching for ways to create greater understanding of the variables that affect organizational success and failure
- Using a diversity of perspectives to develop understanding about organizational issues

A related area of study and practice that has emerged in the last several years also focuses on stakeholder learning from and about evaluation. Often referred to as "evaluation capacity building," evaluators work with organization and community members to develop their evaluation knowledge and skills so that they may conduct evaluations on their own (with or without the assistance of an external evaluator). Building evaluation capacity typically entails developing a system and related processes and practices for creating and sustaining evaluation practice within organizations (Stockdill, Baizerman, & Compton, 2002). (A more in-depth discussion of this topic can be found in Chapter 6.) Since evaluation has become a decentralized function within many organizations, an increasing number of employees are being asked to evaluate their own programs and services (in some sectors, called "self-evaluation"). As a result, employees are increasingly being asked to conduct various kinds of internal program evaluations.

Evaluation has evolved considerably over the last four decades. Reflecting on where evaluation has been, Russ-Eft and Preskill (2001) write,

> Evaluation has grown from being monolithic in its definition and methods, to being highly pluralistic. It now embraces multiple methods, measures, criteria, perspectives, audiences, and interests. It has shifted to emphasizing mixed methods approaches in lieu of only randomized control group designs, and has embraced the notion that few evaluations are value-free and, by their very nature, are politically charged. (p. 46)

Although evaluators have offered a variety of evaluation definitions over years, most would agree that

- Evaluation is a systematic process.
- Evaluation is a planned and purposeful activity.
- Evaluation involves collecting data regarding questions or issues about society in general and organizations and programs in particular.
- Evaluation is a process for enhancing knowledge and decision making, whether the decisions are related to improving or refining a program, process, product, system, or organization, or for determining whether or not to continue or expand a program. And, in each of these decisions, there is some aspect of judgment about the evaluand's merit, worth, or value.
- Evaluation use is of critical importance. Insofar as evaluation constitutes a significant allocation of time and resources, organizations cannot afford to engage in evaluation activities unless the findings are used in some way.
- Evaluation concerns asking questions about issues that arise out of everyday practice.

- Evaluation is a means for gaining a better understanding of what we do and the effects of our actions in the context of culture, society, and the work environment. A distinguishing characteristic of evaluation is that unlike traditional forms of academic research, it is grounded in the everyday realities of practitioners.

Whereas evaluation was once primarily associated with government funded programs, evaluations are now being conducted in every type of public, nonprofit, and private organization, not only to determine a program's merit, value, or worth but also to improve programs, processes, products, systems, policies, and the organization's performance. This growth has not only occurred in the United States but is happening throughout the world. Evidence of this can be seen in the establishment of the European Evaluation Society, Canadian Evaluation Society, the African Evaluation Association, and in the emergence of national evaluation organizations such the Japan Evaluation Society, Australasian Evaluation Society, French Evaluation Society, German Evaluation Society, Danish Evaluation Society, Italian Evaluation Society, Israeli Association for Program Evaluation, Ghana Evaluators Association, Sri Lankan Evaluation, United Kingdom Evaluation Society, Russia International Project Evaluation Network, Malaysian Evaluation Society, and the Nigerian Society for Monitoring and Evaluation, just to name a few. (For more information, see the AEA Web site, www.eval.org.)

## Evaluation in Changing Organizational Contexts

As organizations have merged, reorganized, instituted layoffs, changed leadership, introduced new technologies, and become more globally competitive, evaluators have been challenged to respond to the evolving requirements of those who wish to conduct evaluations. More so than ever before, evaluators are expected to

- Design and implement the evaluation in culturally responsive and appropriate ways
- Be more transparent
- Be performance-improvement and learning oriented
- Practice evaluation in a context of continuous change, that is, where the program being evaluated continues to evolve

This has meant that the role of the evaluator (whether internal or external) has changed and expanded. For example, in the past, evaluators were often thought of as external, "value-free, objective scientists." However, over the years, most have come to understand and acknowledge that evaluation is a highly political activity. And as such, "evaluators are inextricably bound by value commitment and political constraints . . . evaluators are fully situated in the deepest sense: value-imbued, value-laden, and value-based" (House, 2004, p. 7). Thus, in spite of some government requirements to assume a value-free position and conduct randomized control group experiments, many evaluators who are employing more participatory approaches find themselves in the role of educator, facilitator, guide, coach, and technical assistant. Therefore, in addition to understanding basic research design, data analysis methods and approaches, and the development of valid data collection instruments, evaluators also need strong facilitation and communication skills. When working closely with stakeholders, evaluators need to be able to

- Facilitate group meetings
- Negotiate with clients
- Ask good questions
- Listen well
- Be aware of and sensitive to working with multicultural groups
- Understand how adults learn
- Understand how teams develop and function
- Resolve conflicts
- Facilitate dialogue
- Understand organizational culture and change (Preskill & Torres, 1999; Torres, Preskill, & Piontek, 2005).

Perhaps the best way to understand the role of today's evaluators and the wide-ranging set of knowledge and skills that are required can be seen in the list of competencies that have been developed for program evaluators (Stevahn, King, Ghere, & Minnema, 2005; see Figure 2.1).

Even a brief perusal of these competencies confirms that evaluators need much more than research design and data analysis knowledge and skills. Because evaluators work in highly complex, cultural, social, and political environments, and interact with a wide range of stakeholders, there is much to learn.

## Similarities Between
## Appreciative Inquiry and Evaluation

As described in Chapter 1, Appreciative Inquiry is a highly participatory process that addresses issues of importance and concern to an organization. Although AI has been mainly used as an approach to organizational

| 1.0 | **Professional Practice** |
|------|---------------------------|
| 1.1 | Applies professional evaluation standards |
| 1.2 | Acts ethically and strives for integrity and honesty in conducting |
| 1.3 | evaluations |
| 1.4 | Conveys personal evaluation approaches and skills to potential clients |
| 1.5 | Respects clients, respondents, program participants, and other |
| 1.6 | stakeholders |
|      | Considers the general and public welfare in evaluation practice |
|      | Contributes to the knowledge base of evaluation |
| 2.0 | **Systematic Inquiry** |
| 2.1 | Understands the knowledge base of evaluation (terms, concepts, theories, assumptions) |
| 2.2 | Knowledgeable about quantitative methods |
| 2.3 | Knowledgeable about qualitative methods |
| 2.4 | Knowledgeable about mixed methods |
| 2.5 | Conducts literature reviews |
| 2.6 | Specifies program theory |
| 2.7 | Frames evaluation questions |
| 2.8 | Develops evaluation designs |
| 2.9 | Identifies data sources |
| 2.10 | Collects data |
| 2.11 | Assesses validity of data |
| 2.12 | Assesses reliability of data |
| 2.13 | Analyzes data |
| 2.14 | Interprets data |
| 2.15 | Makes judgments |
| 2.16 | Develops recommendations |
| 2.17 | Provides rationales for decisions throughout the evaluation |
| 2.18 | Reports evaluation procedures and results |
| 2.19 | Notes strengths and limitations of the evaluation |
| 2.20 | Conducts meta-evaluations |
| 3.0 | **Situational Analysis** |
| 3.1 | Describes the program |
| 3.2 | Determines program evaluability |
| 3.3 | Identifies the interests of relevant stakeholders |
| 3.4 | Serves the information needs of intended users |
| 3.5 | Addresses conflicts |
| 3.6 | Examines the organizational context of the evaluation |
| 3.7 | Analyzes the political considerations relevant to the evaluation |

**Figure 2.1**   Essential Competencies for Program Evaluators (ECPE)   *(Continued)*

**Figure 2.1** (Continued)

| | |
|---|---|
| **3.8** | Attends to issues of evaluation use |
| **3.9** | Attends to issues of organizational change |
| **3.10** | Respects the uniqueness of the evaluation site and client |
| **3.11** | Remains open to input from others |
| **3.12** | Modifies the study as needed |
| **4.0** | **Project Management** |
| **4.1** | Responds to requests for proposals |
| **4.2** | Negotiates with clients before the evaluation begins |
| **4.3** | Writes formal agreements |
| **4.4** | Communicates with clients throughout the evaluation process |
| **4.5** | Budgets an evaluation |
| **4.6** | Justifies cost given information needs |
| **4.7** | Identifies needed resources for evaluation, such as information, expertise, personnel, instruments |
| **4.8** | Uses appropriate technology |
| **4.9** | Supervises others involved in conducting the evaluation |
| **4.10** | Trains others involved in conducting the evaluation |
| **4.11** | Conducts the evaluation in a nondisruptive manner |
| **4.12** | Presents work in a timely manner |
| **5.0** | **Reflective Practice** |
| **5.1** | Aware of self as an evaluator (knowledge, skills, dispositions) |
| **5.2** | Reflects on personal evaluation practice (competencies and areas for growth) |
| **5.3** | Pursues professional development in evaluation |
| **5.4** | Pursues professional development in relevant content areas |
| **5.5** | Builds professional relationships to enhance evaluation practice |
| **6.0** | **Interpersonal Competence** |
| **6.1** | Uses written communication skills |
| **6.2** | Uses verbal/listening communication skills |
| **6.3** | Uses negotiation skills |
| **6.4** | Uses conflict resolution skills |
| **6.5** | Facilitates constructive interpersonal interaction (teamwork, group facilitation, processing) |
| **6.6** | Demonstrates cross-cultural competence |

Source: "Establishing Essential Competencies for Program Evaluators," by L. Stevahn, J. A. King, G. Ghere, and J. Minnema, 2005, *American Journal of Evaluation, 26,* pp. 49–51. Copyright 2005 by the American Evaluation Association. Reprinted with permission.

development and change, we believe that Appreciative Inquiry and participatory, collaborative, democratic, empowerment, responsive, and learning-oriented approaches to evaluation in particular, share several concepts, values, and goals. (For more information on these evaluation approaches, see Cousins & Earl, 1995; Cousins & Whitmore, 1998; Fetterman, 2001, 2005; House & Howe, 1999; Mertens, 2005; Patton, 1997; Preskill & Torres, 1999; Stake, 2004.) These commonalities include

- Appreciative Inquiry and collaborative forms of evaluation practice emphasize social constructivism whereby participants learn and grow together through asking questions, reflection, and dialogue. Stakeholders' engagement in the inquiry process allows them to co-construct new meanings, which in turn creates a greater level of understanding about themselves, each other, and the focus of the inquiry.

- Appreciative Inquiry and naturalistic, ethnographic, and case study approaches to evaluation use interviews as a primary data collection method.

- Appreciative Inquiry and evaluation are committed to conducting culturally competent and responsive studies.

- Appreciative Inquiry is grounded in storytelling, a common qualitative data collection technique used in evaluation.

- Appreciative Inquiry and learning-oriented forms of evaluation view inquiry as ongoing, iterative, and integrated into organization and community life.

- Appreciative Inquiry and deliberative democratic forms of evaluation value dialogue and strive to be inclusive of many voices.

- Appreciative Inquiry and evaluation practice reflect a systems orientation that includes a structured and planned set of processes.

- Appreciative Inquiry and systems thinking approaches to evaluation both take a whole-systems approach in which they see the context as a dynamic set of relationships and flows of information and resources.

- Appreciative Inquiry and empowerment evaluation both value truth and honesty that comes from participants' experiences and the stories they tell.

- Appreciative Inquiry and most evaluation approaches stress the use of findings for decision making and action.

- Appreciative Inquiry and participatory evaluation approaches recognize and value the importance of language and the impact language has on the process of the inquiry, the ways in which data are collected, and how the results of the inquiry are communicated and reported.

- Appreciative Inquiry and participatory evaluation approaches promote knowledge creation and shared learning among participants, which in turn creates a shared sense of reality.

- Appreciative Inquiry and participatory evaluation approaches strengthen an organization's capacity to be successful; they enable members to be more confident in their decisions, more aware of their options, and better able to focus on results and achievements.

While it is important to note and reflect on these commonalities, we want to make clear that evaluation and Appreciative Inquiry are not one and the same. In other words, AI, as it is practiced for organization development and change, does not necessarily address all of the responsibilities evaluators have to ensure a quality evaluation, such as adherence to the *Program Evaluation Standards* and *AEA Guiding Principles*, use of evaluation logic, or tests of data rigor. Evaluators who use Appreciative Inquiry in their work are still expected to implement an evaluation in a manner consistent with the canons of professional evaluation practice. With this in mind, we believe AI offers evaluators

a. A perspective
b. An approach for conceptualizing and shaping an evaluation
c. A set of tools and strategies for conducting various phases of an evaluation

It is worth noting, however, that the use of AI could also reflect a paradigmatic shift if an evaluation's design and implementation is purposely affirmative and is employed as a means for accelerating the change process.

## Applying Appreciative Inquiry to Evaluation

Appreciative Inquiry can be applied in a wide variety of evaluation contexts and for many different purposes. We have found that the application of AI practices is particularly successful when

- The organization is interested in using participatory and collaborative approaches to evaluation

- An organization's members are open and committed to individual, group, and organizational learning from inquiry

- There is a desire to build evaluation capacity—to help others learn from and about evaluation practice

- The evaluation includes many different stakeholders

- The evaluation must be particularly efficient with regard to time and costs
- The organization values innovation
- The organization is engaged in organizational change and wants to use the evaluation as a means for assessing and preparing members' readiness for change

Interest in the use of Appreciative Inquiry for evaluation purposes has been increasing over the last few years. The following are some brief examples of how evaluators have adapted AI to their evaluation projects:

- Yelton, Plonksi, and Edgerton (2004) used Appreciative Inquiry in an evaluation of the Region A Partnership for Children project, part of the W. K. Kellogg Foundation's SPARK (Supporting Partnerships to Achieve Ready Kids) initiative. The SPARK initiative is intended to create systems-level change for children and families at the local and state levels with the goal of helping children arrive at school better prepared to be successful. As part of the overall evaluation, the initiative's leadership began the process of identifying the vision of how services and relationships would be different for families when conditions were "ideal." This "dreaming" phase of the project was accomplished through community meetings with stakeholders at all levels. Focus groups designed around getting stakeholders to visualize ideal systems for families included electronic audience polling (e-polling) with AI-designed questions. This technology assured inclusion of input from all participants, an instant visual display of audience opinion on each topic for comment and discussion, and automatic recording of data for evaluative purposes. Using Appreciative Inquiry provided valuable and insightful information about both the implementation process and outcomes achieved by the effort.
- Elliott (1999) used an appreciative approach to evaluate programs working with street children in Africa. He first invited stakeholders to participate in a workshop where they were introduced to Appreciative Inquiry. He then developed an appreciative interview protocol. The stakeholders interviewed the street children, analyzed the data, and developed provocative propositions and action plans based on their findings.
- Grayson (2005) used Appreciative Inquiry to evaluate a university's Career Center during a one-day staff retreat. Framing the inquiry around the topic "Incredible Student Outcomes," participants identified specific student learning outcomes and created a vision of what the Career Center would be doing if it were accomplishing the outcomes they envisioned. As part of the *Inquire* phase, staff were asked to tell a story about one success they have had at the Career Center

that brought them great pride in having made a difference for a student or their department. In addition to this core question, questions concerning their values and wishes were also used in the paired interviews. The AI-focused evaluation helped the staff understand the full range of the Center's programs and services that contribute to the identified outcomes. The experience also increased the staff's interest in conducting additional evaluation studies.

- Odell (2002) combined Appreciative Inquiry and participatory evaluation approaches in an effort to evaluate the Habitat for Humanity International's Measuring Transformation Through Houses program in Nepal. Participants in the program developed appreciatively focused planning, monitoring, and evaluation tools, including qualitative and quantitative reports, surveys, and sets of indicators. Collectively, Odell's simplified AI approach to evaluation contributed to generating measures that demonstrated the positive impact that Habitat housing had on families and communities, which, in turn, expedited the building of more homes. The questions that guided Odell's modified AI process were, "What's the best? What's 'even better' look like? How do we get there?" He reports that the process was so enjoyable and empowering that participants gave up their earnings each day to join in the evaluation process (which he calls a-valuation; personal communication, July, 2005).

- Mohr, Smith, and Watkins (2000) conducted an evaluation of a simulation-based training program at SmithKline Beecham Pharmaceuticals using AI to help focus the evaluation and to develop interview protocols. The client's core team also helped analyze the data from 100 interviews and co-wrote the evaluation report.

- McNamee (2003) used Appreciative Inquiry to evaluate a secondary school department's curriculum and the faculty's ability to work collaboratively. In a three-day retreat, faculty first participated in the *Inquire* and *Imagine* phases where they told stories, discussed their values and wishes, and described their ideal curriculum. On the second day, they participated in the *Innovate* phase, which resulted in five plans for an ideal curriculum. The retreat concluded with the *Implement* phase where the faculty discussed how to operationalize the program they imagined. By the end of the retreat the faculty had a plan for taking four immediate steps.

Determining when and how much AI to use for an evaluation most likely depends on the answers to a number of questions. For example, is the client willing to involve a large number of stakeholders in the evaluation? How committed is the client to learning from the evaluation and using the evaluation's results? What experience does the client organization have with Appreciative Inquiry? And, what is the client's experience with evaluation? There may be situations in which the client is interested in using AI but has no personal experience, and thus may be timid about using it. In these cases, it may be wise to engage the client in a brief Appreciative Inquiry session.

## Incorporating Appreciative Inquiry Into Evaluation Practice

In the following chapters we describe three specific ways that AI can be successfully used to design and implement an evaluation, and to build organization members' evaluation capacity. These include the following:

1. *To focus an evaluation and to develop an evaluation plan*—Most evaluations are guided by a plan that is developed by the evaluator after significant discussions with the client. As will be explained further in Chapter 3, this plan includes information about the program's history, its goals and objectives, the evaluation's stakeholders, key evaluation questions, data collection and analysis methods, a timeline and other project management plans, and a budget. AI's *Inquire* and *Imagine* phases are most helpful for collecting much of this information. And, if time is available to add the *Innovate* phase, participants are able to co-construct a program logic model that further describes the program's underlying assumptions, resources, activities, and short- and long-term objectives. Appreciative Inquiry can be a particularly effective approach to obtaining information for the plan since it involves a wide range of stakeholders, helps participants understand the evaluation's purpose and the intended uses of the findings, and because it is a positive approach to addressing an evaluative issue.

2. *To design and conduct interviews and surveys*—Appreciative Inquiry's *Inquire* and *Imagine* phases can be used to design interview and survey questions to be more appreciative. Chapter 4 discusses the difference between positive and appreciative questions, describes ways in which questions can be reframed and designed, and provides examples of appreciatively oriented interview guides and surveys.

3. *To design an evaluation system*—Appreciative Inquiry's *Inquire, Imagine, Innovate,* and sometimes *Implement* phases can be used to develop an evaluation system. Using AI in this kind of work engages stakeholders in the process of identifying and creating an evaluation system based on what is currently in place and what is working or has worked in the past. Chapter 5 explains how this can be accomplished, and presents case examples of how Appreciative Inquiry has been used to develop an organization's evaluation system.

An advantage of applying AI to evaluation is its infinite flexibility—it may be used simply to pose one appreciative question, or it may be used to reframe an entire evaluation process. Yet, regardless of how AI is used for evaluation purposes, it ultimately contributes to building organization members' evaluation capacity (Chapter 6).

## Summary

As described in this chapter, evaluation has continually evolved as new questions have been raised, as organizations have changed, and as evaluators have searched for new and effective ways for enhancing the quality of their work and the use of evaluation results. Using Appreciative Inquiry in evaluation fosters a fresh and positive view of evaluation because it is more engaging, illustrates possibilities, and creates hope for a better future. As a result, Appreciative Inquiry may (a) increase the richness of the data collected, (b) help the evaluator obtain important contextual and stakeholder information, (c) increase the efficiency of the data collection process, (d) increase participants' level of trust and participation in the evaluation, and (e) respect the diversity of participants' experiences and opinions.

Furthermore, as participants learn more about their program through the appreciative process, they also develop evaluative thinking (e.g., how to construct a program logic model, how to design evaluation questions, how to identify best methods) and appreciative thinking (e.g., how to study success, understanding the role of storytelling and active listening, and the importance of language). They are able to reframe their perspectives about evaluation and may be more willing and able to support and engage in future evaluation studies. In this way, they are more likely to use the evaluation's results for decision making and action. In the end, we believe that applying Appreciative Inquiry to evaluation adds a new dimension that makes evaluation more effective. The following chapters provide detailed guidance and illustrations of how AI processes can be used to design and implement evaluations in a wide variety of organizational and community contexts.

# Focusing the Evaluation Using Appreciative Inquiry

# 3

> *You will never leave where you are, until you decide where you'd rather be.*
>
> —Dexter Yager

One of the most useful and exciting applications of Appreciative Inquiry is in the Focusing Phase of an evaluation. In the Focusing Phase, the evaluator collects as much information about the program as possible, in order to develop an evaluation plan that will guide the evaluation's implementation. This chapter first describes eight essential components of an evaluation plan. It then discusses how Appreciative Inquiry can be used to facilitate a Focusing Meeting and provides a sample agenda that can be modified to a variety of evaluation purposes and circumstances. To illustrate how AI has been used to conduct a Focusing Meeting and to develop an evaluation plan, three case examples, each highlighting a different evaluation context, are included.

## Developing an Evaluation Plan

As explained in Chapter 2, evaluation is a planned and systematic process. Thus, an evaluation needs to be carefully designed to ensure that (a) it will collect credible and useful data, (b) the client's information needs will be met, and (c) the evaluation resources will be wisely used. Accordingly, most evaluators develop an evaluation plan that outlines in significant detail why, how, where, and when the evaluation will be implemented. The time spent developing the evaluation plan is often referred to as the *Focusing Phase*, which is then followed by the *Implementation Phase* of the evaluation. Ideally, the *Focusing Phase* should result in

- Agreement between the evaluator and the client concerning why the evaluation is being conducted,
- Agreement between the evaluator and the client regarding the expected deliverables from the evaluation (e.g., a verbal presentation, executive summary, comprehensive written report),
- The client's understanding of and commitment to using the evaluation's findings, and
- The client's commitment to support the evaluation actively.

For external evaluators in particular, an evaluation plan may also serve as the contractual agreement between the evaluator and the client. The most useful evaluation plans tend to include the following information (see Figure 3.1).

## 1. Background of the Program and Rationale for the Evaluation

This section of an evaluation plan typically describes (a) the history of the program being evaluated, including how it came into being, (b) its funding sources, (c) the individuals or groups commissioning the evaluation, and (d) the factors that have led to the need for or interest in the evaluation. This information helps ground the need for the evaluation and clarifies the evaluation's purpose and key questions.

---

**Evaluation Plan Information**

- Background of the program and the rationale for the evaluation
- Program logic model
- Evaluation purpose statement
- Evaluation stakeholders
- Evaluation key questions
- Evaluation approach or model, data collection and analysis methods
- Timeline and other project management plans
- Evaluation budget

---

**Figure 3.1**    Evaluation Plan Components

## 2. A Program Logic Model

A program logic model is a visual tool for describing how a program (or process, or system) is supposed to work based on its theory of action and desired outcomes. In developing the logic model, evaluators guide stakeholders through a process where they reflect on and identify (a) the underlying assumptions of the program, (b) the program's activities, (c) the resources needed to deliver and sustain the program, and (d) the program's short- and long-term objectives and outcomes. Some logic models also include possible outputs and impacts of the program. In effect, "the Logic Model is the basis for a convincing story of the program's expected performance" (McLaughlin & Jordan, 1999, p. 66). A logic model is extremely useful for helping stakeholders identify and discuss various elements of the program's purpose and expected outcomes. This process often articulates implicit goals, and surfaces competing assumptions, inaccurate information, and common understandings—all of which are vital for determining the focus, breadth, and scope of the evaluation.

## 3. Evaluation Purpose Statement

An evaluation purpose statement is a two- to four-sentence statement that succinctly describes the reason(s) for the evaluation and how the results will be used. It ensures that everyone involved in the evaluation is clear about why the evaluation is being conducted. For example, an evaluation's purpose might be "to make decisions about the program's improvement, continuance, expansion, or certification, or to monitor a program's implementation for compliance. Other purposes might include obtaining evidence of a program's success to build support for additional resources, or gaining a better understanding of the program's effects on different groups" (Russ-Eft & Preskill, 2001, p. 136). The purpose statement is derived from information gained about the program's background and the rationale for the evaluation.

## 4. Evaluation Stakeholders

In large part, evaluation is conducted to serve the interests and information needs of a wide range of stakeholders. By definition, a stakeholder is an individual or group who has a "stake" or vested interest in the process and outcome of the evaluation; stakeholders are also referred to as the "intended users of evaluation findings" (Patton, 1997). Not all stakeholders, however, have the same kinds of information needs. That is, different individuals and groups may wish to know more or less, or different things about the evaluation's progress and its results. Therefore, it is useful to categorize stakeholders into three groups: primary, secondary, and tertiary. *Primary* stakeholders are often those who fund the program and/or are ultimately responsible for the program's implementation and continuation. This group might include program staff, managers, executives, and funders. *Secondary* stakeholders are typically more removed from the daily operations of the program, but still have an important interest in the program and the outcome of the evaluation. This group might include program administrators, students or participants, customers or clients, staff, parents, vendors, donors, and governing boards. *Tertiary* stakeholders are those who have some interest in the evaluation for future planning or decision making or have some general concern or right to know the evaluation's results. These stakeholders might include potential users or adopters, community members, legislators, future participants, and organizations that are interested in the program. There are no hard and fast rules that define whether a stakeholder is primary, secondary, or tertiary—it always depends on the context of the organization, community, and evaluation, and is best determined through negotiation with those commissioning the evaluation.

The following questions may help identify the evaluation's stakeholders:

- Who has a vested interest in the program and in the outcome of the evaluation?
- Whose position could be affected by the evaluation's findings and actions taken on the findings?
- Who cares about the program?
- How might the evaluation findings be used and by whom?
- What groups will be affected by the evaluation if recommendations are made and acted upon?
- Who are the clients or customers of the program and what stake might they have in the outcomes of the evaluation?
- Who has a "right to know" the results of the evaluation? (Russ-Eft & Preskill, 2001, pp. 142–143)

As implied in these questions, it is expected that stakeholders will use the evaluation findings in some way. When evaluators talk about *use of evaluation findings,* they are usually referring to three kinds of use. The first is called *instrumental use* and occurs when stakeholders act on a recommendation or a result soon after an evaluation, and the action can be seen or heard. This type of use often happens in formative evaluations where the results are used to make refinements and improvements to the program. The second type of use, *conceptual use,* refers to a situation where the reader of the report, or listener to a verbal presentation, integrates the evaluation findings with other information he or she may have gained from other sources and experiences, and consequently may come to a new understanding about some aspect of the program. While they may not make any immediate decisions, or take any actions based on the evaluation's findings, these stakeholders may apply what they learned from the evaluation in future decisions and actions, or the findings may simply change their perception or level of understanding about the program. *Symbolic* or *persuasive use* refers to the third type of evaluation use and occurs when evaluation findings are used to lobby for resources; persuade others of the need for program expansion, reduction, or elimination; or are used to merely report that the evaluation took place. It is likely that for any one evaluation, the findings will be used in multiple ways.

When an evaluation plan is being designed, efforts should be made to identify all of the possible stakeholders and to consider whether they are primary, secondary, or tertiary relative to their intended uses of the evaluation findings. The results of this conversation will provide insights into the evaluation key questions and the ways in which the findings may be communicated and reported during and after the evaluation.

## 5. Evaluation Key Questions

The evaluation's key questions are the broad, overarching questions that frame the evaluation and communicate the scope and boundaries of the inquiry. Key questions are generally open-ended and are used to determine which data collection methods will best address the client's information needs. In addition, the evaluation's key questions guide the development of data collection instruments such as surveys and interview guides.

## 6. Evaluation Approach or Model, Data Collection and Analysis Methods

In this section of an evaluation plan, the evaluation's overall approach and specific methods for collecting and analyzing data are described. For example, evaluators may choose to use a utilization-focused approach (Patton, 1997) combined with an organizational learning approach (Preskill & Torres, 1999) because they want to emphasize both using the evaluation findings and the desire to have those involved in the evaluation learn from the evaluation process and its outcomes. Or, an evaluator might use an objectives-oriented approach where the focus is on the extent to which a program has achieved its objectives. (For more information on various evaluation models and approaches, see Fitzpatrick, Sanders, & Worthen, 2003; Owen & Rogers, 1999; Posavac & Carey, 2003; Rossi, Lipsey, & Freeman, 2004; Russ-Eft & Preskill, 2001). The choice of which approach or model to use in conducting an evaluation influences the desired level of stakeholder involvement, the evaluation's design, and the ways in which data will be collected. Commonly used data collection methods include

- Individual or focus group interviews (in-person or by phone or computer)
- Surveys (mailed, online, telephone)
- Observation (participant or non-participant; qualitative, quantitative; video, photographs)
- Document and record review (archival data)
- Tests (paper, computer-based)

As indicated earlier, the choice of which data collection methods to use should be based on the evaluation's key questions. That is, one should look at each question and determine which method(s) will most effectively address the questions in ways that are appropriate, feasible, and acceptable to the organization and its members. For each method chosen, the evaluation plan should include information on the population (data sources); the sample size and sampling procedures (if necessary); how, when, and where the data will be collected; how the data's validity will be ensured; and how the data will be analyzed. Evaluation plans may also include drafts of the data collection instruments (e.g., survey, interview guide, observation form, test).

## 7. Timeline and Other Project Management Plans

Developing a variety of management plans helps keep the evaluation project on time and on track. Such plans might include

- A timeline for implementing the evaluation
- An outline of each evaluation task and who is responsible for implementing the task
- A matrix that matches the evaluation's key questions with the data collection methods and sources
- Suggested strategies for addressing challenges to the evaluation's implementation should they arise
- A communications plan that describes how each stakeholder group will be contacted and consulted during and/or after the evaluation (see Torres, Preskill, & Piontek, 2005, for a comprehensive treatment on strategies for communicating and reporting)

## 8. Evaluation Budget

Evaluation plans almost always include a budget for designing and implementing the evaluation. Evaluation budgets normally include costs for

- Personnel (evaluator, clerical support, subject matter experts, consultants)
- Materials, supplies, and equipment
- Communications (e.g., phone, postage)
- Technology (e.g., Internet and Intranet costs, software)
- Printing and copying
- Travel
- Facilities
- Overhead and/or general administration
- Miscellaneous or contingency costs

Once the evaluation plan has been developed and approved by the client, the *Implementation Phase* of the evaluation commences. This phase includes the development or completion of the data collection instruments, selecting the sample (if necessary), collecting and analyzing data, developing recommendations (if requested by the client), and designing communicating and reporting processes and products.

# The Focusing Meeting

To collect information for the evaluation plan, the evaluator usually meets one-on-one with the client, or possibly with a few of the program staff, for a couple of hours to discuss the program and their reasons for wanting to conduct the evaluation. While this meeting can result in greater clarity for the evaluator, it often falls short of providing the quantity and quality of information needed to write a comprehensive evaluation plan. Furthermore, such a meeting does not necessarily reflect an inclusive approach, in that the information provided is likely limited to the few people in the room. In our view, a more collaborative and effective approach is to ask the client to invite a group of 4–12 stakeholders to participate in a *Focusing Meeting*. In most cases, these individuals would have some responsibility and/or involvement with the program being evaluated. They may be program designers, managers, vendors, clients, parents, students, program staff, community members, and/or officials who have an interest in the program and its evaluation. The important point is to ensure a diversity of perspectives and experiences relative to what is being evaluated. The resulting group may be called an Evaluation Task Force, Evaluation Advisory Committee, Evaluation Working Group, Evaluation Steering Committee, or Evaluation Team. The role of the group is to provide guidance, feedback, and support of the evaluation's design and implementation. In some cases, this group might also be asked to collect data and to assist in the data analysis. When inviting these individuals to participate, it is essential that they (a) understand the importance of their role, (b) understand that they may be asked to review evaluation related documents, and (c) attend a few meetings throughout the implementation of the evaluation (depending on how much their participation is desirable and possible).

Once the group has been invited, the next step is to schedule the *Focusing Meeting*. It is essential that an adequate amount of time be allocated for collecting the necessary information at this meeting. The length of the meeting generally depends on the complexity of the evaluation, the political nature of the program being evaluated, the number of people attending the meeting, and practical considerations regarding time and scheduling. The significance of this meeting cannot be overstated, since much of the evaluation's success will depend on the evaluator's understanding of the program's context, the purpose of the evaluation, and the stakeholders' intended use of the results. Involving stakeholders in this process may take more time, but doing so increases the likelihood that (a) participants will have a greater commitment to the evaluation, (b) participants will learn more about the program and evaluation practice, (c) more useful data will be collected, and (d) the evaluation resources will be well spent.

## Using Appreciative Inquiry to Focus the Evaluation

Evaluators may use any number of strategies to engage participants during a *Focusing Meeting*. For example, they may simply discuss each of the evaluation plan's components in an open dialogue. Or, they might use other group process approaches such as brainstorming (Eitington, 2001), nominal group technique (Harrington-Mackin, 1994), force field analysis (Bens, 2000), or Ideawriting (Moore, 1994). The chosen approach usually depends on the evaluator's personal style and level of facilitation skills, and on the cultural context and preferences of the organization and its members.

While the above mentioned approaches can be fairly effective in gathering information for the evaluation plan, using Appreciative Inquiry to focus an evaluation offers several important benefits. It

- Creates greater levels of participant understanding and commitment to the evaluation process
- Creates common understandings about the program

- Provides more in-depth information
- Increases participants' creativity and innovation in addressing the evaluation topic
- Increases the likelihood that the evaluation's findings will be used
- Can be more cost and time efficient

Using an AI approach may also counter some participants' negative perceptions of evaluation in that it establishes a different kind of atmosphere—one that is focused on successful experiences and on creating a more positive future. As a result, participants often feel less threatened and resistant to participating in and supporting the evaluation. Furthermore, appreciative questions invite participants to share useful information about the program's logic and theory, underlying values, and ideas for improvement. More detail on the nature of appreciative questions is presented in Chapter 4.

While useful information can be collected during a *Focusing Meeting* in as little as two hours, it is preferable to allocate between four and eight hours if at all possible. Asking people to devote a half or full day to this effort represents a considerable amount of time, and clients might bristle at this request. However, if the goals of the meeting are to ensure that everyone understands the program and its intended effects and outcomes, and to determine the evaluation's purpose, key questions, and intended use of findings, then a strong case can be made that such a meeting is actually more efficient (both in terms of time and costs) than other approaches for obtaining this information. Furthermore, if the evaluator decides to explain that an Appreciative Inquiry approach will be used, he or she can fully articulate the importance of allowing sufficient time for the paired interviews, sharing of stories, and visions that are likely to emerge from this meeting. It might help if the client understands that the meeting is actually a data collection activity that will not only help shape and guide the evaluation but that it is also a unique opportunity for stakeholders to get to know each other and the program better, and for them to have a voice in the future of the program.

## The Focusing Meeting Agenda

A *Focusing Meeting* can employ Appreciative Inquiry in a number of ways. Figure 3.2 shows a sample *Focusing Meeting* agenda that includes time estimates, activities, and required materials. Based on the client's particular expectations and requirements, time available, and the organization/evaluation context, the agenda can be easily adapted and modified.

The total time for implementing the agenda ranges from two hours (if the optional activities are excluded and the minimum amount of time is adhered to) to eight hours (if all of the activities are implemented at the upper range of the times noted). As can be seen in Figure 3.2, the meeting begins with an icebreaker activity, introductions, an explanation of the

| Minutes | Activity | Materials |
|---------|----------|-----------|
| 10–60 | • Ice breaker activity<br>• Introductions<br>• Purpose of the meeting<br>• Meeting agenda<br>• Introduction to Appreciative Inquiry | • Ice breaker materials<br>• Handouts:<br>　o Agenda<br>　o Information on AI<br>　o Slides (overview of AI) |
| 45–90 | • *Inquire*—Best practices, examples of success | • Handouts:<br>　o Interview questions<br>　o Notes page for interviewer<br>• Flip-chart paper and markers for each table |
| 30–60 | • *Imagine*—Vision of the program's future—use of evaluation findings and recommendations | • Handout:<br>　o *Imagine* discussion question<br>• Flip-chart paper and markers for each table |
| 45 | • *Innovate*—Develop provocative propositions (*useful for developing the program's logic model*) | • Handouts:<br>　o Elements of an organization's social architecture<br>　o Guidelines for writing provocative propositions<br>• Sticky notes or 3 × 5 cards<br>• Flip-chart paper on which sticky notes or cards can be posted |
| 60 | • Develop program logic model | • Flip-chart paper, markers<br>• Sticky notes |
| 30–60 | • Develop evaluation key questions (using data from the *Inquire* and *Imagine* phases) | • Sticky notes or 3 × 5 cards<br>• Flip-chart paper |
| 30 | • Identify stakeholders | • Flip-chart paper, markers |
| 30 | • Discuss potential data collection methods (*optional*) | • Flip-chart paper, markers |
| 5–15 | • Summary and wrap up<br>• Questions and answers | |

**Figure 3.2**    Sample Focusing Meeting Agenda

meeting's purpose and agenda, and a brief introduction to Appreciative Inquiry. Based on the organization's experience with AI and how much time is available, the evaluator might choose to eliminate the overview of AI. If participants want to know more about Appreciative Inquiry, the evaluator/facilitator can provide this information at a later time.

Once introductions have been made and the purpose of the *Focusing Meeting* is made clear, participants are asked to pair off and to interview each other for a number of minutes. This activity reflects the *Inquire* phase of AI and is extremely effective for illuminating participants' best practices, examples of success, the values they have about themselves and the program, and their wishes for achieving more instances of success. After the interviews and sharing of their stories in small groups, each group reports the themes of its stories to the larger group.

The next activity is to have groups of six or eight participate in a discussion about the program's future based on an *Imagine* question. This question asks group members to create a vision for the program's future that is grounded in their past successful or peak experiences. Once the groups have discussed these and have flip-charted their themes and shared them with the larger group, it is time for the *Innovate* phase. If time is short, there may not be time for this phase. If there is, participants are asked to develop provocative propositions that reflect the organization's social architecture and to write them on sticky notes. It is a good idea to provide a few examples and some guidelines for how to write these statements since this part of the AI process is often the most challenging for participants. Once participants have developed several provocative propositions, they are asked to place them on flip-chart paper affixed to the wall, next to others that reflect similar ideas. When everyone has posted his or her notes, several themes will have emerged. The evaluator/facilitator then asks the participants to label these themes, which he or she writes on the flip-chart paper. This phase of the process is particularly useful since participants develop provocative propositions that describe, in concrete terms, what the program is doing when its success has been achieved (a vision of an operationalized future). The resulting statements typically reflect the program's activities and resources as well as its short- and long-term goals, which is an excellent lead-in to developing the program's Logic Model if there is time available.

The data produced from the *Inquire* and *Imagine* phases are rich with insights about what the program looks like when it works well. This information can then be used to develop the evaluation's key questions. To do this, participants would be asked to do the following:

*Think about our earlier discussion of best experiences regarding this program and your wishes for making the exceptional high points the norm, as well as your visions for moving constructively into the future. Now consider the following questions:*

- *What questions should the evaluation address, so that you have the information needed to help you move toward your desired future?*

- *What do we (the evaluators) need to know so that you can experience more peak experiences and successes?*

*Write one question on each sticky note. Write succinctly and legibly. The questions can be broad or specific. Think about the ideas noted in your vision, and your wishes for having more peak experiences like those from your stories.*

After an appropriate amount of time, participants begin to post their questions on the flip-chart paper posted on the wall. The evaluator/ facilitator might ask participants to group these, identify themes, and even prioritize which questions are most critical to address now versus later.

Again, if there is time, participants should be asked to identify the various stakeholders for the evaluation and how they might use the evaluation findings. They might also be asked a series of questions about the organization's experiences with various data collection methods, which methods might be most effective and well received, and what relevant and accessible data already exist within the organization.

A summary of what has been learned during the meeting is a good way to bring the meeting to a close. The evaluator could describe what will happen with the data participants generated, how the data will be used to develop the evaluation plan, and when a draft of the plan will be available for their review (depending on the evaluator's work guidelines).

While it may be tempting to acquiesce to clients who say they can only commit to an hour or 90 minutes for the *Focusing Meeting,* it is worth considering what is lost by not giving adequate time to the sharing of stories and participants' values and wishes. In these cases, it might be better to ask only one appreciative question and then have a more traditional open dialogue or brainstorming session. In other words, if the evaluator tries to implement the *Inquire* and *Imagine* phases too quickly, everyone might end up more frustrated and disillusioned with the process and outcomes, which might limit the usefulness of the resulting data and lead to an unfair perception of Appreciative Inquiry.

## Case Examples of Using Appreciative Inquiry to Focus an Evaluation

This section presents three case examples that illustrate how Appreciative Inquiry practices were used to focus an evaluation and develop an evaluation plan. Each demonstrates a variation of using AI based on the particular evaluation circumstances and organizational context. For example, in the case of the New Mexico Coalition of Sexual Assault Programs, only the *Inquire* phase of AI was used, whereas in the case of the Evergreen Cove Holistic Learning Center's evaluation, both the *Inquire* and *Imagine* phases were used to design the evaluation plan. The third case example illustrates how three appreciative questions from the *Inquire* phase can be used to frame an evaluation plan even when the interviewees are in different geographic locations.

## Case Study 3

### Evaluating the Training Provided by the New Mexico Coalition of Sexual Assault Programs (CSAP)[1]

To develop the evaluation's focus, the evaluators used only the *Inquire* phase of Appreciative Inquiry to generate information for the evaluation plan.

### Background

The goal of the Coalition is to offer child sexual abuse and sexual violence prevention programs, and to advocate for safe communities throughout the state of New Mexico. The Sexual Violence Prevention Program focuses on providing training sessions to school personnel, parents, students, and service providers that address the following topics: (a) how to identify child sexual abuse, (b) the protocol for responding to child sexual abuse, (c) the use of the child sexual abuse prevention resources and activity manuals, and (d) State and Federal sex crime statutes. It is believed that through training and education, participants will become more aware of sexual violence issues, and with that knowledge, they will be empowered to make changes within the community response system. Another aspect of this program is to identify and train individuals as rural prevention specialists who are expected to build sexual violence prevention capacity in the community by providing ongoing training and education. The Director of Training had been the primary provider of the training sessions for the last several years. She was often contacted by a person in the community requesting her to conduct a training session (sometimes called a "workshop") for one of the four identified groups.

The training was expected to have the following short-term outcomes:

- Children, youth, and teens learn prevention techniques for avoiding sexual assault.

- Sexual assault victims learn how and where to report such incidents.

- Sexual assault myths and stereotypes diminish.

- Knowledge about appropriate response to, investigation of, medical/forensic examination of, prosecution of, and treatment of sexual assault victims among community response professionals increases.

- Public is sensitized to issues of sexual assault, abuse, and other forms of sexual violence.

- Public becomes more comfortable talking about issues related to sexual violence.

Although training in these communities had been provided for several years, little evaluation data had been collected. In response to the state's requirement that all of its contractors conduct evaluations of their funded programs, an evaluation was commissioned. The findings from the evaluation were to be used to determine future program planning efforts.

*(Continued)*

(Continued)

### The Evaluation Advisory Group

In concert with the Coalition's desire for the evaluation to be collaborative, participatory, and learning-oriented, 15 people were personally invited by the executive director and trainer to participate as Advisory Group members. These individuals, who are Hispanic, Native American, and Anglo, were selected because of their involvement with a variety of the Coalition's initiatives and the belief that they would provide valuable insights into the evaluation plan's development.

### Deciding to Use Appreciative Inquiry to Focus the Evaluation

The evaluators learned that while Advisory Group members were familiar with the program, they did not know each other, and their experiences with the program varied significantly. As a result, the evaluators decided that engaging Advisory Group members in a dialogue about the program and asking them questions about effectiveness would not be terribly productive since they shared no common experience with the training program. Instead, the evaluators believed that using an Appreciative Inquiry approach would not only help people meet and connect with one another, but that it would be a way for them to highlight what they did know about the program and what their visions were for the program if it were successful. The evaluators and the Coalition's Executive Director and Director of Training invited the Advisory Group members to a one-day meeting to help focus the evaluation and to develop the evaluation plan.

### The Focusing Meeting

The meeting began at 10 a.m. and ended at 4 p.m. (box lunches were provided during a 40-minute lunch break). The following describes in detail how the meeting was facilitated.

*10:00–10:15 Welcome*

The Coalition's Executive Director made some introductions and thanked everyone for agreeing to be a member of the Evaluation Advisory Group. She explained why the evaluation was being conducted, how the results would be used, and why they were invited as Advisory Group members.

*10:15–10:35 Hello and Overview of the Day*

The evaluators introduced themselves and provided an overview of the meeting goal, which they had written on a piece of flip-chart paper:

To collect information from Advisory Group members that will be used to develop an evaluation plan of the New Mexico Coalition of Sexual Assault Programs.

Recognizing that the Advisory Group members had little background in evaluation, the evaluators had developed a laminated poster that described the major components of an evaluation plan. They briefly described each of the components and explained that the participants would be involved in a process that would provide information for developing the evaluation plan.

*10:35–11:10 Advisory Group Introductions*

Most of the Advisory Group members did not know each other, so it was important to find out about each other and their roles relative to the Coalition's work. Participants were asked to introduce themselves by describing where they were from, their role with the Coalition, specifically as it relates to training on sexual assault prevention, and why they agreed to participate in the evaluation process.

*11:10–11:30 Appreciative Interviews (Inquire)*

Advisory Group members were asked to pair up and were then provided a handout with three interview questions. They were told that they should spend 10 minutes interviewing each other (20 minutes total) and that they were to take notes on their partner's story. They were asked to listen carefully to each other's words and not to interrupt unless it was to gain clarification or more information.

The New Mexico Coalition of Sexual Assault Programs is committed to providing education and training throughout New Mexico on treatment and advocacy specific to sexual violence issues. The goal of the project is to increase the number of victim services advocates throughout the state by providing training and various educational materials.

In pairs, interview another person using the following questions:

1. Take a moment to think about your work with Coalition over the last several months. Remember a particular moment or time when you knew that what you were doing on behalf of the Coalition was having a significant impact. You were excited by this realization and were proud of what you were doing. You had the intense feeling that you (Coalition) were making a difference in the lives of people with whom you interacted. Describe this peak experience. Where were you? What were you doing? Who else was there? What was the context? Why did you feel or think this way?

2. If the Coalition wanted to ensure that you had more of these positive, energizing experiences, what resources would be particularly important for making this happen?

3. Without being humble, what do you most value about yourself with regard to the work you do with the Coalition?

*11:30–11:50 Appreciative Interviews—Sharing Stories*

The pairs were then asked to join one or two other pairs and for each person to tell the highlights of their partner's story and values. The groups were asked to listen and note any themes they were hearing across the interviews and to write these on pieces of flip-chart paper.

*11:50–12:10 Large Group Debrief on Themes and Core Values*

Each group was asked to report out the themes they had noted on their flip-chart paper.

*(Continued)*

(Continued)

*12:10–12:50 Lunch*

*12:50–1:30 Developing the Evaluation's Purpose Statement*

Based on their positive past experiences with Coalition, and specifically the training it provides rural communities, the evaluators asked the Advisory Group members to consider what the purpose of the evaluation should be. They were prompted to complete the following statement:

The purpose of the evaluation is to: _____.

The following are the purpose statements they created as a large group:

- Measure the quantity and quality of the impact of trainings on community providers.
- Measure the effects of the training on participants and community.
- Present information on how CSAP is having a positive impact on the community.
- Document the effectiveness of training and collaborative efforts.
- Determine the impact of rural child sexual abuse trainings.
- Identify sexual assault prevention program effectiveness.
- Determine the impact of training—tools to ensure training in remote/rural areas.
- Measure the impact of child sexual abuse training on criminal investigation and prosecution.

After some discussion and clarification about the training workshops, the following purpose statement was agreed upon:

The purpose of the evaluation is to explore the ways in which training has affected participants' ability to address sexual violence issues and services in two New Mexico communities.

*1:30–2:30 Developing Evaluation Key Questions*

Participants were asked the following question: "If you could ask three to five questions about the Coalition's effectiveness and impact, what would they be?" They were then asked to pair up again, and each pair was given five sticky notes on which they were asked to write one question on each. Once the questions were written, participants were asked to place them on pieces of flip-chart paper at the front of the room. They were told to group the questions on the sticky notes next to ones with similar content. This process generated approximately 51 questions. The evaluators read each question out loud, asked for clarifications, and then asked participants to identify a label for that question. The end result was eleven categories under which one to ten questions were placed. The evaluators then facilitated a discussion about which categories (and questions) were most important for the evaluation. In other words, with limited resources, it would be impossible to answer each question. The results of this conversation led to the group agreeing to eliminate two of the categories. The group was also told that the evaluators would use their questions to develop the final evaluation key questions to be included in the evaluation plan.

*2:30–3:00 Wrap-Up*

The meeting concluded with the evaluators summarizing what had been accomplished and explaining that they (the evaluators) would soon be asked to review a draft of the evaluation plan that would include the evaluation's rationale, purpose, key questions, evaluation design, data collection methods, timeline, and budget.

**Next Steps**

The evaluators took all of the information generated on the flip-chart pages and sticky notes and developed a draft of the evaluation plan, which they later submitted to the Advisory Group members and the Coalition staff for their review. They incorporated the few suggested revisions into the final version of the evaluation plan.

**Value of Using Appreciative Inquiry in the Focusing Phase**

The Coalition staff and Advisory Group members believe that using AI to focus the evaluation had several following benefits. In particular, they thought AI

- Helped group members get to know each other quickly and respectfully in order to do the necessary work. Through the sharing of their stories, it valued individuals' cultural traditions and differences.

- Helped quieter individuals feel welcome and involved from the start.

- Created a common experience even though as individuals, they interact with the Coalition in very different ways. The use of Appreciative Inquiry helped them co-create another story about the wide range of effects the program may be having.

- Was an effective way to gain an understanding of the program's scope of service and the critical issues it faces.

- Was a cost effective way of gathering a great deal of data in a very short period of time. Had the evaluators attempted to individually interview Advisory Group members and Coalition staff, it would have been much more expensive, and it is likely that they would not have collected the quality and depth of information that resulted from using Appreciative Inquiry.

The Coalition staff found this process so productive and engaging that they have since presented this experience at professional conferences.

## Evaluating a Two-Year Appreciative Inquiry Initiative of an Alternative Health Center[2]

To focus the evaluation of the Evergreen Cove's change process, the evaluator used the *Inquire* and *Imagine* phases of AI. A complete description of the change management process using Appreciative Inquiry is described in the appendix.

### Background

Evergreen Cove Holistic Learning Center (EC), founded by Sarah Sadler in 1993, provides alternative health solutions to its community members on Maryland's Eastern Shore of the Chesapeake Bay. As Sadler prepared to retire in 2003, Evergreen Cove launched an Appreciative Inquiry to help initiate the next phase of its mission while preserving the uniqueness of its culture. In late 2004, as the impact of the Appreciative Inquiry continued to unfold throughout the community, Evergreen Cove launched an evaluation of its appreciative transformation process. An independent evaluator in collaboration with EnCompass LLC, Potomac, MD, conducted the evaluation. From this evaluation, the organization hoped to record, understand, and appreciate the impact of its transformation process.

### The Focusing Meeting

Because AI was used to facilitate the change process, it made sense to also use Appreciative Inquiry for the evaluation. To launch the evaluation, a group of people met to focus the evaluation. This included the external evaluator and a leadership group comprised of Evergreen Cove founder Sadler, its current executive director, a member of the board, and the AI consultant who facilitated the two-year AI process. The purpose of the focusing meeting was to

- Reflect on exceptional changes and practices

- Conduct a stakeholder analysis

- Develop a vision

- Determine the evaluation's key questions

The leadership group had two concerns about the evaluation: (1) it did not want the evaluation to have a negative effect on the emerging citizens' initiatives sparked by the Appreciative Inquiry change process; and (2) it worried that using a more traditional quantitative evaluation approach would miss the depth and breadth of the Appreciative Inquiry's impact. The committee hoped that by embedding an appreciative approach into the evaluation, it would have a higher chance of capturing what had happened over the life of the change process and, as a result, would have more meaning for the community. In addition, taking an appreciative approach would be consistent with the values and philosophy of the change process.

The meeting began with appreciative interviews in response to the following interview questions:

1. Reflect for a moment on your involvement with Evergreen Cove since the Board and Provider Retreat in January 2003 and think of all the changes Evergreen Cove has gone through since that time. Remember a peak experience—a significant change that stands out for you, a change in which you felt most involved, most engaged, or most proud of your work or engagement with Evergreen Cove. Tell a story about that change.
   a. What happened? Who was involved? What did you contribute to the experience? What were the key factors that made it possible? Tell your story describing the experience in detail.

2. What do you most value about the contribution of Evergreen Cove to the community and to the world?

3. If you had three wishes for the continued evolution of Evergreen Cove's work in the community and in the world to make more of these peak experiences possible, what would they be?

Participants responded to these questions with significant enthusiasm. They became aware of the broad and daring dimensions of the AI change initiative's goals. These goals included a wish to be assisted in their transition from the founding leadership to a new generation of leadership, a wish to broaden its sense of community, reaching new, diverse membership, and growth through collaboration with the community health system. They wanted to pursue these goals while preserving Evergreen Cove's identity and sense of values. Interestingly, the group quickly became aware of the magnitude of the transformation they had sought through the AI. They had already achieved an increased level of respect with the health system in the community, including new funding from the county health department, new relationships with underserved people in the community, and continued communication and sharing of Evergreen Cove's values with its growing membership. They were supporting and tracking the efforts of four "Healthy Communities Initiatives" that had resulted from the Appreciative Inquiry process.

The focusing session resulted in concrete goals for the evaluation. Specifically, Evergreen Cove wanted the evaluation to help them monitor (a) how well they were keeping the change initiative going, (b) how well they were maintaining their values throughout this process, (c) the extent to which they were gaining credibility with donors and community members, (d) how they could continue to build momentum and become a "showplace for the possible," (e) how well they were meeting the needs of clients and staff, and (f) how they might craft a future that is sustainable through fundraising and the exploration of "resilient communities."

From their appreciative interviews and dialogue, the leadership group identified the following key evaluation questions that were used to design and implement the evaluation:

- What are the core values of those involved in the Healthy Communities Initiative?

(Continued)

(Continued)

- How well has Evergreen Cove been listening to its stakeholders regarding the changes it has been making?
- How successful has Evergreen Cove been in fundraising and diversifying its funding base with new donors?
- How successful has Evergreen Cove been in developing new partnerships? What format have these partnerships taken?
- How inclusive has Evergreen Cove been in its transformation process?

By the end of the focusing meeting, the leadership group members were excited about the evaluation and the information it would produce.

### Reflections on the Use of Appreciative Inquiry

The evaluation succeeded in documenting a transformation that had occurred within the Evergreen Cove organization, the community, and its stakeholders. The findings that were summarized in a final report have enabled Evergreen Cove to see itself in a new light. So many changes had been going on that it had been difficult for anyone to know all of them and to appreciate the extent of everyone's efforts. One of the most significant contributions of the evaluation was the logic model that the evaluator developed, which explicitly linked the goals, strategies, and activities of the change initiative. Using the appreciative questions at the focusing meeting helped the leadership group members reflect on the ambitiousness and complexity of the Healthy Communities Initiative. In so doing, they were able to develop a clear sense of purpose and direction for the evaluation. Even though the leadership group initially questioned whether an evaluation would be able capture the richness of the changes and the magnitude of their accomplishments, they discovered that the evaluation process actually helped clarify the internal logic of their endeavor, and that led to an evaluation report that included a much stronger narrative and more useful information for the organization.

### Case Study 5

### Evaluating Knowledge Sharing and Capacity Building in Education for the World Bank[3]

This case study illustrates how the use of Appreciative Inquiry was adapted to accommodate the logistical constraints of a team of participants who were geographically dispersed and on different travel schedules.

### Background

In 2002, the United Kingdom Department for International Development (DFID) funded a three-year research, analysis, and dissemination activity to help countries participate in the knowledge economy. The overall goal of the studies was to provide tools and knowledge to enable developing countries to make informed policy choices for reforming post-basic education and to strengthen training systems to meet the challenges of lifelong learning. The World Bank was selected to implement the studies with DFID funds that were placed into a Trust Fund. In three years, the Trust Fund sponsored 21 studies, which tackled a range of topics including distance education in South Asia, guidance and counseling in Eastern Europe, and teacher skills assessment in sub-Saharan Africa. An additional goal of the DFID–World Bank collaboration was to share knowledge between the two donors in order to inform their international education funding programs.

At the end of Year 2, the Trust Fund commissioned two evaluations: one to synthesize the findings of the 21 studies and assess the degree to which these studies produced innovation in post-basic education; and the second, to determine (a) the impact and extent to which the donor organizations were sharing their knowledge, (b) the impact of DFID and the World Bank's collaborative relationship with regard to the research being conducted, and (c) the impact of the research studies on education policy reform in the countries where they were conducted. This case example describes the second evaluation that focused on the collaboration and knowledge sharing between the two donors.

### Planning the Focusing Process

To focus the evaluation, a "planning group" of stakeholders was defined. The planning group included four managers: two *current* managers (one at DFID and one at the World Bank) and two managers who had established and managed the Trust Fund for its *initial* start-up period, but were no longer working with the Trust Fund. The initial managers had had more extensive involvement with the work of the Trust Fund, while the new current managers were in charge of managing the third year of the project, which was devoted to disseminating the results of the research studies. These four managers were identified as the stakeholders who should be involved in focusing the evaluation since the initial managers had important background information and history with the project, and the current managers would ultimately be responsible for using the evaluation results.

While it is almost always preferable to bring together a group of stakeholders who can collaboratively plan the evaluation, it is sometimes the case that bringing people together in one location is not feasible, as was true in this situation. Due to their heavy travel schedules, it was not possible to bring the four managers together for a *Focusing Meeting*. Thus, in order to obtain the information needed to develop the evaluation plan, the evaluator conducted individual interviews with the four managers—two face-to-face (the two World Bank managers in Washington, DC) and two by telephone (the DFID managers in London).

### Deciding to Use Appreciative Inquiry

The evaluator decided to incorporate AI into the *Focusing* phase of the evaluation because she believed it would illuminate important benefits of the project, and

*(Continued)*

---

**(Continued)**

---

because the evaluation's goals included identifying ways in which the outcomes of the project could be effectively disseminated and shared in the third and final year of the research program.

The interview guide that was developed to focus the evaluation included questions that concerned the managers' understanding of the goals and scope of the DFID–World Bank collaboration, the two institutions' perspectives regarding the purpose of the evaluation, and the issues and concerns of each manager regarding the evaluation. Since the managers had little to no experience with Appreciative Inquiry, and the evaluator thought it was important to include appreciatively oriented questions, she developed an interview guide that included both AI questions and non-AI questions. (For more information on designing interview guides, see Chapter 4.) The interview guide was structured in the following way:

- General questions on person and institutional perspectives (Questions 1–3)

- Specific questions regarding the accomplishments of the studies related to collaboration, knowledge sharing, and capacity building (Questions 4–6)

- Appreciative Inquiry questions (peak experience, wishes, vision) (Questions 7–9)

The interview guide included the following questions:

1. What, in your view, has been the greatest achievement of the Trust Fund (TF)?

2. What has been the role of DFID in the Trust Fund, beyond providing funding?

3. What is the unique contribution of the Trust Fund to education research?

4. What products (knowledge and tools) have come out of this project? How have they been disseminated?

5. What partnerships with other agencies have been built through this collaboration?

6. What has surprised participants the most over the course of this collaboration?

7. Think back on your experience managing the Trust Fund, and tell me a moment when you felt more excited and proud to have been part of the Trust Fund. What was going on? What was happening at headquarters, in the field, and with the partner donor agency?

8. Based on your best experiences with the TF, what are some wishes you have for how the TF might have more exceptional experiences?

9. In your eyes, what would it look like "to have achieved the objectives of the collaboration"?

The resulting interview data highlighted the wide range of familiarity the managers had with the research studies conducted by the Trust Fund. The managers' responses pointed out that the emphasis of the first two years was in setting up the TF, collaborating with regional scientists to solicit proposals for studies, and administering these studies. Consequently, the resulting evaluation plan was designed to learn as much as possible about collaboration, knowledge sharing and capacity building from each of the studies, and effective ways to disseminate the research findings in Year 3.

Because of the structure of the Trust Fund and its natural evolution, each of the four managers interviewed had very different types and levels of involvement in the Trust Fund operations. Asking the appreciative questions enabled even the least involved managers to describe an aspect of the Trust Fund's collaboration with the World Bank where they experienced success that was energizing to them, and the questions helped them suggest ways in which the Trust Fund could build on its current successes for the future (in its third year). In fact, despite very different experiences with the Trust Fund, the managers' views converged in terms of their wishes for the future. These centered on knowledge sharing and the dissemination of findings and reflection with a wider audience. The appreciative questions also provided an opportunity for everyone to express their hopes in terms of the desired outcomes of the third year.

**Reflecting on the Use of Appreciative Inquiry**

Although the data from the interviews were meaningful and useful for developing the evaluation plan, it is true that conducting individual rather than paired or group appreciative interviews prevented the managers from hearing each other's stories. During the individual interviews, the evaluator tried to convey some of the key points and enthusiasm of each person interviewed to the others. This still did not have the same impact as having participants engage in paired interviews, as is usually done when implementing an Appreciative Inquiry process. Using the appreciative questions did, however, help the managers provide a direction for the evaluation that was more constructive than it might have been had another process been used. Since all four managers were inclined to discuss their deficiencies and what they did not do, it would have been difficult for the evaluator to discover the wide range of accomplishments of the Trust Fund without the appreciative questions.

# Summary

This chapter has highlighted the use of Appreciative Inquiry for focusing an evaluation and for developing an evaluation plan. Used in this context, AI helps illuminate participants' peak experiences and successes, which ultimately provides insights into the evaluation's purpose, key questions, design, and implementation. Since Appreciative Inquiry is a collaborative and participatory process, participants learn more about themselves, each other, the program's explicit and implicit goals and logic, the organization, and, ultimately, about evaluation practice, right from the beginning of the inquiry. Referred to as "process use" (Patton, 1997), this kind of learning from the evaluation process is immensely valuable for supporting current and future evaluation studies. Another critical outcome is that participants often develop a sense of ownership of the evaluation—and responsibility for its success. Using Appreciative Inquiry to focus an evaluation also builds confidence that the evaluation can, indeed, be a constructive process that moves the program in the direction of a desired future. After participating in a *Focusing Meeting*, stakeholders are better able to see how evaluation is closely linked to strategic planning, learning, and effective decision making.

## Notes

1. The evaluation was conducted by PRISM Evaluation Consulting Services, Albuquerque, NM. Reprinted with permission.

2. The evaluation was conducted by EnCompass LLC, Potomac, MD. Reprinted with permission.

3. The evaluation was conducted by EnCompass LLC, Potomac, MD. Reprinted with permission.

# Designing and Conducting Interviews and Surveys Using Appreciative Inquiry

# 4

> *It is not the answer that enlightens, but the question.*
>
> —Eugene Ionesco

At the heart of Appreciative Inquiry is the power of appreciative questions to change those who ask them and those who answer them. With AI, getting the questions right is the most important part of the inquiry. When appreciative questions are crafted well and asked with integrity, they invite participants to begin a journey of discovery that leads to increased trust, learning, and constructive change. In fact, sometimes, even one appreciative question in an evaluation can change the whole evaluation experience. This is true whether AI is used in focusing an evaluation (as described in Chapter 3) or in later data collection efforts. This chapter describes how AI can be applied to the data collection process and how it can be used to shape the design of interview guides and surveys. Even if Appreciative Inquiry is not used in the *Focusing Phase* of an evaluation, it is still possible and useful to frame or reframe interview and survey questions appreciatively. Doing so may

- Provide richer information about the program or organization's context

- Reduce the development of leading questions

- Create greater trust between the evaluation participants and the evaluator

- Reduce evaluator bias (real or perceived)
- Produce results that are easier for stakeholders to accept since the language used is less negative and threatening
- Reduce evaluation participants' fear about the evaluation process and how the results may be used
- Result in more meaningful and useful data
- Yield more positive outcomes and achievements with less time and effort

In this chapter, the difference between *appreciative* and *positive* questions is discussed, underscoring the point that appreciative questions not only energize respondents, but that they may also result in more meaningful and useful data. In describing how and when appreciative questions can be designed and used for conducting interviews and surveys, several examples are provided to illustrate the various kinds of questions and formats.

## The Nature of Appreciative Questions

Those who are considering using Appreciative Inquiry in evaluation are often concerned about a perceived "positive bias" that might result from asking appreciatively oriented questions. In part, this anxiety stems from clients who ask how valid it is for the evaluation to focus only on the *positive*. If *positive* and *appreciative* meant the same thing, this would be a legitimate concern. By definition, however, these words represent related but different concepts. The word *positive* is defined as "Marked by or indicating acceptance, approval, or affirmation; marked by optimism; contributing to or characterized by increase or progression" (*Merriam-Webster's Collegiate Dictionary*, 2003). By definition, to *appreciate* is "To grasp the nature, worth, quality, or significance of; to value or admire highly; to judge with heightened perception or understanding; to recognize with gratitude; and to increase the value of something" (*Merriam-Webster's Collegiate Dictionary*, 2003). Thus, questions such as, "What did you enjoy most today?" or "What do you like about your manager's supervision style?" which ask respondents what they liked about a program (rather than what they did not like), or to explain what they liked about their manager's supervision style (rather than what they do not like), are questions that lead the respondent to positive answers. Without asking respondents about any negative perceptions, these questions could indeed create a positive bias in the participants' responses.

Appreciative questions, however, are not simply about asking people what they liked, or how things looked from a positive perspective. Appreciative questions ask respondents to communicate their concept of the nature, worth, quality, and significance of a program or some aspect of the organization. Moreover, they ask respondents to honor the past while expressing gratitude for, and pride in, their achievements. And, the appreciative *wishes* questions invite respondents to share their ideas for how to increase the value of the program. Hence, the role of appreciative questions is not to learn what respondents liked, but rather to focus on the study of successful moments that can be used to grow and improve the program in the future.

The choice of studying success rather than problems and gaps is grounded in the image-action connection described in Chapter 1. That is, the mind cannot develop a negative image or negate a picture—for example, the statement "do not paint this blue" makes us see blue; we do not have the ability to imagine "not blue." Therefore, since humans have a tendency to move toward the images they hold, when studying problems, the mind will focus on negative mental images, and our thoughts and actions will reinforce those images. Conversely, when studying successful experiences, the power of the positive images shared and studied will move participants toward thoughts and behaviors that make them successful. So, instead of thinking of questions as positive or negative, AI focuses on developing questions that

- Aim to identify and study moments of excellence
- Solicit information regarding successful processes and outcomes in connection to what is being evaluated
- Invite respondents to build on this information to provide feedback and insights on what should be done in the future to move toward improved outcomes

Appreciative questions inquire into successful instances even if they are the exception to the norm in a system. As a result, they identify the life-giving forces in the program or organization. This is why appreciative questions ask for stories, values, wishes, visions, and detailed plans for the future. For these reasons, in designing interview and survey questions, the emphasis is on the study and analysis of successful processes and outcomes rather than on problems and their causes.

## Determining the Role of Appreciative Inquiry in Interviews and Surveys

The purpose of using AI in designing an interview guide or survey is to allow the evaluator to collect data about participants' peak experiences with the program and to explore the factors that have contributed to those successes. In determining the extent to which AI should be incorporated into an interview guide or survey, the following should be considered:

- *The purpose of the evaluation and the evaluation's key questions.* As with all evaluations, the evaluation's design and choice of data collection methods should be closely aligned with the questions the evaluation is seeking to answer.

- *The nature of the program being evaluated.* Certain evaluation designs and methods are better able to elicit information in a trustworthy and respectful manner than others. Appreciative Inquiry is well suited for situations in which people may be afraid to talk about certain subjects because of its emphasis on successful experiences. Hearing others' stories or reading the results from an appreciative process allows participants to give and receive difficult messages more easily.

- *How open the client is to using Appreciative Inquiry.* There may be cases when the client's limited experience with AI influences how much of the appreciative approach may be used.

Because evaluators work in a wide variety of contexts and settings, and with diverse sets of stakeholders, there are situations when the evaluator does not have complete control over an evaluation's design or data collection methods. These include the following:

- An interview guide or survey has been approved after a lengthy review process, and the evaluator is brought in after the interview guide or survey has been designed

- A client wants to use an existing interview guide or survey that has been used in previous evaluations

- The evaluator wants to develop a fully appreciative interview guide or survey but is part of a larger evaluation team whose members want to develop an instrument using non-AI questions

- The client is inexperienced in using AI and wants to introduce it into the organization slowly, thus permitting only one or a few appreciative questions to be included on the interview guide or survey

Regardless of any limitations on how much Appreciative Inquiry can be used in designing and conducting interviews and surveys, including even one appreciative question is better than asking no appreciative questions, because it can still benefit the evaluation process.

# Designing and Conducting Interviews Using Appreciative Questions

For questions that seek answers concerning individuals' experiences and perspectives, evaluators often rely on interviews, which they hope will produce data that are rich with examples, stories, and insights. In general, interviews

- Allow the interviewer to make a personal connection with the interviewee, which often enhances the quality and quantity of the data provided

- Often result in useful and important information about the evaluation's context and setting

- Provide opportunities to obtain data from people who have difficulty reading and writing

- Can allow unexpected information to surface—information for which questions are difficult to develop in advance

- Provide opportunities for participants to interact with one another in ways that may enrich the depth and quality of the data (during group interviews)

Interviews can be conducted one-on-one in person or over the phone, in small groups, or online. They typically last from 10 to 90 minutes but can be longer depending on the number of questions, the purpose of the interview, and the type of interview. (For more information on conducting interviews, see Patton, 2002; Rubin & Rubin, 2005.) Given that Appreciative Inquiry is grounded in storytelling, using AI to reframe and design interview questions is particularly relevant and beneficial for evaluation purposes.

Incorporating appreciative questions regarding interviewees' peak experiences or successes, values, and wishes (*Inquire* phase) into an interview guide provides a means for interviewees to consider and provide feedback on when their program has been successful—when it has worked at its best. By adding a vision question (*Imagine* phase), interviewees are able to provide suggestions for how the program can move to a higher level of performance, while also offering creative and innovative ideas for achieving their images of the future.

## Formulating Appreciative Questions

Because appreciative interview questions focus on instances of success, peak experiences, values, and wishes, they tend to look and feel very different from non-AI questions. For example, consider the following:

An evaluator was contracted to determine the effectiveness of a training program's (1) design, (2) relevance to participants' jobs, and (3) influence on participants' ability to transfer their learning to their jobs. In addition to other data collection efforts, the evaluator decided to conduct individual interviews with the training program's participants. She drafted two sets of interview questions—one of non-AI questions and one that was more appreciative in stance and tone.

## 1. Training Program Design

*Non-AI Questions:* How well did the workshop balance small group activities and large group discussions? Were the case studies useful? Why or why not? What would have made the case studies more useful?

*Appreciative Questions:* Think back on your experience in the workshop and tell me about a moment when you felt that an activity or lecture was working particularly well—so well that it helped you learn and understand the content in a way that was exciting or inspiring. What was it that made it so effective? What value did you add to the workshop? If the entire workshop were designed to be this clear, interesting, and engaging, what three wishes would you offer the workshop's designers to make that possible?

## 2. Relevance of Workshop Content

*Non-AI Questions:* How relevant was the workshop content to your work? Which topics were particularly relevant? Which topics were not relevant? Of the topics covered, which ones did you already know about?

*Appreciative Questions:* Again, reflecting on your experience in the workshop, remember a topic that you thought was particularly relevant to your work. What topic was it? Why was it relevant to what you do? If this workshop were designed to be totally relevant and useful to your job, what additional topics would it include?

## 3. Transfer of Learning

*Non-AI Questions:* Was it worth your time going to the workshop? What are some examples of how you might apply some of the things you learned? Who else might benefit from this workshop?

*Appreciative Questions:* It has been several weeks since you participated in the workshop. You find that since you've returned to your daily responsibilities, you are referring to things you learned or people you met that day. What parts or aspects of the workshop are you finding to be most useful in your work? What have you used that has been particularly effective, successful, or exciting? What do you wish the workshop had included more of to make it even more useful?

The benefit of the appreciative questions, as described in the above example, is that they take participants through a process of reflection that invites them to examine their successes and to identify ways for improving the workshop. While both non-AI and appreciative questions are structured to seek helpful information, the appreciative questions may elicit more detailed and valuable information by focusing on the participants' stories of success and the best moments of their workshop experience, in addition to providing realistic recommendations for future offerings. And, because appreciative questions incorporate the criteria respondents use to judge the workshop's effectiveness, their responses are grounded in their positive experiences rather than some abstract notion of what they liked or what they assume they should have liked. Finally, those who designed and delivered the training will find this feedback meaningful and specific, and they will gain insight into a particular part of the training that they have also experienced as a trainer, but this time, from the participants' perspectives.

## Interviewing Options Using Appreciative Inquiry

Appreciative Inquiry can be used to design and conduct interviews in three ways:

1.  Individual interviews (face-to-face or via telephone)

2.  Group interviews without a paired interview component

3.  Group interviews with a paired interview component

### Individual Interviews

Conducting open-ended face-to-face and telephone interviews are effective methods of collecting qualitative data that result in stories, opinions, attitudes, and examples of people's experiences. An interview guide might include only appreciative questions, or appreciative questions may be embedded with other non-AI questions, depending on the needs of the client and the evaluation. Although conducting individual interviews (rather than paired interviews) can result in relevant and highly useful data, it should be noted that from an Appreciative Inquiry perspective, the interview data may not be quite as insightful and the process will not be as energizing for the interviewees, since they will not have the opportunity to hear others' stories.

---

**Case Study 6**

**Conducting Phone Interviews to Evaluate the Training Provided by a State Education Agency[1]**

This case example describes how twenty interviews were conducted using an interview guide that included both AI and non-AI questions.

*(Continued)*

(Continued)

## Background

The National Center for Education Statistics, U.S. Department of Education, provides each state education agency with funding to hire a state coordinator to serve as a liaison between the state and the National Assessment of Educational Progress (NAEP). Key tasks of NAEP state coordinators include implementing and coordinating NAEP activities in the state, promoting understanding of NAEP and its relevance to the state, enhancing state capacity to use NAEP data, and promoting assessment literacy. Fifty-three states and jurisdictions have NAEP state coordinators. The NAEP State Service Center provides ongoing support, technical assistance, and training for NAEP state coordinators; responds to information requests regarding NAEP; and maintains a NAEP Information Center. The NAEP State Service Center also provides NAEP coaches, who are assigned to coordinators to provide individual support.

The senior evaluation specialist for this project worked closely with an evaluation work group of NAEP State Service Center and National Center for Education Statistics staff to design the evaluation. Data collection for the 2003–2004 evaluation included NAEP state coordinator surveys for each NAEP State Service Center training event; individual interviews with NAEP coaches, a random sample of 20 NAEP state coordinators, and key NAEP State Service Center staff; and exit interviews with NAEP state coordinators who had left their positions.

Although NAEP state coordinators complete evaluation surveys for each in-person training event, the evaluation work group agreed that it was important to conduct individual interviews with a sample of coordinators to allow for more in-depth responses regarding in-person training, and to gather additional information related to other training and support provided by the National State Service Center (NSSC). The interviews were designed to focus on

- Additional training and support needs
- Preferred delivery methods for training and support
- Perceptions of the effectiveness, usefulness, and appeal of current training and support
- How coordinators have used the knowledge, skills, and materials gained from training and support
- How training and support have contributed to NSSC outcomes

## Using AI in the Interview Guide

Because traditional survey questions had been previously used to evaluate each of the in-person trainings, the evaluator decided to take a different approach in developing the protocol for the NAEP state coordinator interviews. She wanted to obtain new information from the coordinators—in particular she wanted to document the strengths and best practices of the NSSC, so that the NSSC could build on those strengths. At the same time, there was a need to address several specific questions that the NSSC wanted answered. The resulting interview protocol was a mix of appreciative questions and non-AI questions.

Twenty NAEP state coordinators, who were randomly selected, were invited to participate in one-hour phone interviews. The following questions guided the interview:

*Orientation Process*

1. Please describe the orientation process you've been through as a NAEP state coordinator. What are the strengths of this process?

*Training—Training Events, Pre-Release Workshop, Web Seminars*

2. What are the two or three most effective, useful, and appealing NSSC training experiences you've had as an NAEP state coordinator? What were the key factors that helped make them successful for you?

3. If you had three wishes that would ensure that every NSSC training experience would be as good as the ones you just described, what would they be?

4. What types of training do you find most effective and appealing (e.g., workshops, WebEx)?

5. Please give me two or three specific examples of how you've used knowledge and skills gained from NSSC training.

6. In what ways have you disseminated each state's results?

7. What are you most looking forward to learning about for your job as a NAEP state coordinator?

*Support Materials and Products—State Guide to NAEP Participation, Orientation CD, Presentation Templates, etc.*

8. Which support materials and products have you used most often? Why did you choose them? How did you use them?

9. What additional materials and products would be useful to you? In what format should they be delivered?

*Individual Support—Coaches, Help Desk/Information Center, Support for Secondary Analysis, Support for Public Access to Secure Items*

10. What type of individual support do you most often seek and why?

11. Please provide two or three specific examples of how individualized support has helped you in your job.

*Other*

12. What are your needs and your state's needs regarding NAEP Network meetings?

13. In what way(s) could the NSSC be most helpful to you now?

**Benefits of Using Appreciative Questions**

The appreciative questions gave the NAEP state coordinators the opportunity to reflect on their own learning, to identify their personal learning styles and preferences, and to articulate their learning goals as they relate to their job. In addition,

*(Continued)*

---

**(Continued)**

these questions were framed in a way that made the coordinator the focus, not the NSSC or the evaluation. Consequently, the interviewees seemed more comfortable, engaged, and direct when responding to interview questions.

When analyzing the data from the interviews, the evaluator found that the themes emerged more clearly from the responses to the AI questions. For example, for some of the non-AI questions, responses sometimes became a laundry list of items or examples with little to no organization. The AI questions, on the other hand, required the coordinators to reflect before responding, to think before speaking. This resulted in more focused and organized responses, which made for easier and more accurate data analysis and subsequent identification of key themes. Furthermore, the interviewees' responses to the appreciatively worded questions were similar in format to the wording of recommendations. With data from more traditional interview questions, the evaluator often has to translate findings about what didn't work into recommendations for what would work, or simply phrase the recommendation as what "not" to do. Because the coordinators' responses to the AI questions were already framed in terms of what would work for them, the recommendations flowed easily from their data.

While it is possible that similar information could have been obtained from non-AI worded questions, using the appreciative questions made it easier for coordinators to thoughtfully and clearly talk about what had worked for them in the past, what would work for them in the future, and what they want to learn for their job. As a result, the quality of the interview data was richer, and the resulting findings and recommendations were much more useful.

As this example demonstrates, even when it is not possible to implement paired interviews or use a completely appreciative interview guide, even asking a few appreciative questions can enhance both the interviewee's as well as the interviewer's experience, and the value and depth of the resulting data.

---

## Case Study 7

### The Impact of Using One Appreciative Question to Evaluate a City Health Department[2]

This case example illustrates a situation where the evaluation team was only able to add one appreciative question to an already developed interview guide that included other non-AI questions.

#### Background

The District of Columbia Department of Health (DC DOH) commissioned an evaluation to determine what improvements were needed to help the DC DOH take on its emerging role of moving out of direct health service delivery and into a role of planning, policy development, and quality assurance. Soon after developing an interview guide using non-AI questions, the evaluation team (made up of evaluators and department staff) learned about Appreciative Inquiry and decided to add the following appreciative question to the beginning of the interviews with DC DOH staff: *Tell me about a time in the last year when you have been particularly proud of the work you are doing—a time when you felt most committed to the DC DOH.* The remainder of the interview guide included questions about the problems that staff members were facing, their level of compliance with job descriptions and standards, their ideas of how various processes could be redesigned, and the systems that needed to be developed.

**Conducting the Interviews**

Once the evaluation was completed, the 15 evaluators who had conducted a total of approximately 60 individual interviews reported how the one appreciative question had changed the tone of the interviews and the usefulness of the resulting data. The evaluators admitted that they had gone into the interviews somewhat critical of the client as a result of the D.C. government's recent takeover by an independent board. As a result, the city employees' morale was extremely low. The appreciative question that sought information about interviewees' successes resulted in the DC DOH staff sharing their own passion for their clients (D.C. residents), and the ways in which they had gone above and beyond the call of duty to make DC DOH work in difficult times. This not only energized the DC DOH staff, but hearing their stories enabled the interviewers to see the staff in a more positive light, which resulted in their resolve to contribute constructively to DC DOH's future through this evaluation.

**Benefits of Using Appreciative Inquiry**

This example also demonstrates that one not need employ the full AI process, nor ask many appreciative questions to benefit from an application of Appreciative Inquiry for gathering important and useful information. At a time when the D.C. city services were under attack across departments, starting the interviews with a study of exceptional service by DC DOH staff, respondents were able to reveal some of the critical strengths in the system, and how they had employed those to provide exceptional service. The department staff that conducted the interviews began with a negative bias about the city services. As a result of conducting the interviews, however, this perception shifted dramatically. Using the appreciative question helped them hear information in a way that non-AI questions would not have been able to ask or address.

## Group Interviews Without a Paired Interviews Component

An often-used method in evaluation practice is the focus group interview. This type of interview involves 6–12 individuals who are invited to participate in a group interview because of their common experience with the program being evaluated. The goal of the interview is to obtain information regarding the range of opinions, attitudes, and perspectives concerning the evaluation topic. As such, a focus group interview is not concerned with reaching consensus, nor is it about brainstorming solutions to a problem. (For more information on conducting focus group interviews, see Krueger & Casey, 2000.) When it is not feasible for participants to conduct paired interviews, it is still possible to use an appreciative interview guide within a focus group setting.

---

**Case Study 8**

## Conducting Focus Groups to Evaluate
## the Girl Scouts Beyond Bars Program[3]

In this next case, Dawn Smart describes how her evaluation team conducted two appreciatively oriented focus group interviews within the context of a larger evaluation of the Girl Scouts Beyond Bars (GSBB) program, which serves daughters of women inmates at the Washington Corrections Center for Women (WCCW) and women preparing for release at the Tacoma Pre-Release Center (TPR).

The program's theory of change is that the girls involved—through participation in challenging learning activities with peers, appropriate guidance and emotional support from adults, and the opportunity for increased contact with their mothers—will resist engaging in at-risk behavior, including future involvement in crime. The activities of GSBB are those customarily associated with scouting, focused on character building; but the heart of the program is building the connection between girls and their mothers. The program combines traditional community-based Girl Scout troop activities and field trips with Corrections Center–based scout meetings involving both mothers and daughters. The 3-year evaluation of GSBB tracked progress toward four long-term outcomes identified by the Girl Scout councils:

1. Greater involvement of girls with caring adults

2. Increase in girls' positive peer relationships

3. Increase in girls' sense of connection to the community

4. Preserved and enhanced relationship between girls and their mothers

The mixed method evaluation design included record review, structured observations of meetings, surveys of girls and mothers, focus group interviews, and telephone interviews with a sample of girls' guardians. In the third year of the evaluation, two focus group interviews using appreciative questions were conducted with the girls and the Girl Scout staff and leaders. We decided to include appreciative questions to see if we could uncover additional indicators of program success or areas that needed improvement. We also chose to take an appreciative stance because we thought it would be a good fit with the asset-based scouting program and the participatory approach of the evaluation. And we opted to conduct focus group interviews since they had been done in the previous two years of the evaluation (without the appreciative questions), and our experience with AI had shown the value of people's interaction in the process—how one story or example of "the best" generated others, and how the sharing of ideas about what to take into the future could be inspiring to the group.

One focus group interview was conducted with 14 girls who were participating in the program as a part of the monthly Girl Scout meeting. A focus group interview with four Scout staff and leaders followed a few weeks later. The interviews began with a brief explanation that we were collecting information to learn more about the program and their experiences with it. The interview guide for both groups included the following four questions:

1. Tell a story or give an example that shows what's best about this Girl Scout troop.

2. Consider the stories and examples you just heard—what did they have in common?

3. What circumstances or conditions made these "exceptional moments" possible?

4. What phrase, motto, song lyric, or advertising jingle might capture the themes just discussed that you want to take with you into the future?

Because of the nature of these questions, they flowed seamlessly from one to the next. Highlights from the participants' stories and examples were posted on flip-chart paper and in written notes. When the groups discussed common themes from their stories in response to the second and the third questions, these were also posted on flip-chart paper. Participants had little trouble distilling the common themes from the stories and examples and thus required little prompting or assistance from the facilitator.

The comfortable and informal atmosphere seemed to create an enjoyable experience for the focus group interview participants. Consequently, there was a high degree of participation in both groups, although this was especially true in the girls' group, where the age range was from 7 to 16. Although a few girls in the group were quiet, volunteering little even if called on, they were attentive and followed the conversation without distraction throughout the meeting. Given the positive nature of the interview questions, the process was an uplifting one—in the girls' group there was considerable laughter and giggling as stories were shared, and in the staff and leaders' group there was a clear sense of gratification and passion communicated through stories.

### Benefits of Using Appreciative Inquiry

The use of appreciative interview questions for the focus group interview proved to be a good decision for the evaluation. It provided us with a better understanding of what was most meaningful about the program from its primary stakeholders–participants, Girl Scout staff, and volunteer leaders. The personal stories and examples clarified the girls' experiences, and allowed them to describe them in ways that were meaningful. The themes identified from the appreciative interview questions were closely aligned with the long-term outcomes identified for the program and confirmed much of the other data collected for the evaluation. Obtaining additional and different insights from these questions complemented and added to the data collected through conventional methods, proving especially useful in soliciting data on program quality and helping to validate the program's theory of change.

The Girl Scout councils have continued the Girl Scouts Beyond Bars program, expanding the number of girls participating each year. The program remains focused on building the connection between girls and their mothers and building supportive relationships between the girls and the adults, and their peers involved in the program, both of which were at the top of the list of common themes identified from the appreciatively oriented focus group interview.

### Group Interviews With a Paired Interview Component

Another option for conducting interviews using Appreciative Inquiry is when the evaluator has the opportunity to work with a group of program participants or organization members, and is provided the time and resources to implement the full AI process. In these situations participants engage in paired interviews (*Inquire* phase) and then participate in the remaining AI phases through large group questioning and discussion (*Imagine, Innovate, Implement*).

The following case example demonstrates how the results of three focus group interviews that used appreciative questions led to the development of an online survey that was later used in the evaluation.

---

**Case Study 9**

## Conducting Focus Groups for the Evaluation and Usability Review of the World Bank's Intranet[4]

As part of a larger evaluation, three two-hour focus group interviews were conducted with approximately 50 employees in the World Bank's Information Solutions Group (WB ISG), using a fully appreciative interview guide. The purpose of the evaluation was to understand the impact of the Intranet on staff performance and the effectiveness of the Intranet from a usability standpoint.

**Conducting the Group Interviews**

After a brief introduction, participants conducted paired interviews with three questions that focused on (1) an exceptional experience that involved the Intranet to enhance their job performance, (2) what they value most about their work, and (3) their wishes for how the Intranet could be most useful for enhancing their job performance (*Inquire*):

- Reflect for a moment on your involvement with the Bank's Intranet, and remember a peak experience or a high point—a time when you felt most satisfied by its use, either because you were proud of an aspect that you helped design or launch, or because, by using it, you were able to accomplish an important task more efficiently. Tell me a story about that time.

- What happened? Who was involved? What did you contribute to the experience? What were the key factors that made it possible? Tell your story describing the experience in detail.

After conducting their interviews, participants identified themes and developed visions of the Intranet's exceptional contributions to productivity using the following question (*Imagine*):

Imagine that you are 5 years in the future, and the new design of the Intranet has been rolled out to great success. The president has selected you for an award for your excellent work! What does the new design look like? Why is it so successful? What are WB staff saying about it? What does your internal newsletter say about you? List the reasons that the new design was so successful and describe in detail the thoughts, feelings, and experiences associated with the revamped Intranet.

The participants' visions indicated that the ideal Intranet would include robust functionality including a strong search engine, access to email when traveling, efficient links with hand-held devices, simple and easy-to-navigate architecture, a warm and inviting look-and-feel, rich and integrated content, and buy-in from the staff.

Based on the themes identified in their interviews, and their visions for the Intranet, participants developed provocative propositions with the following prompt (*Innovate*):

Think about the WB staff's everyday work processes and systems that would benefit the most from a revamped Intranet (as presented in the vision), so that the efficiency and effectiveness of these work processes would really improve. Write down the work processes where you expect to see improvement first.

The purpose of this particular task was to clarify which work processes participants thought should be targeted for improvement in the immediate future. Once their responses were collected and discussed, respondents were asked:

What questions would you like to ask WB staff in order to best understand their views and priorities for how the Intranet could be revamped to best serve their work needs?

Responses to this question were used to develop a follow-up online survey to obtain feedback from WB staff on those elements that the interviews suggested were most important for achieving their vision and provocative propositions.

### Benefits of Using Appreciative Inquiry

Results from the individual and group interviews were synthesized and presented in a summary report. This intermediate report along with the results from additional individual staff interviews, the usability tests, and the online staff survey were incorporated into a comprehensive final evaluation report. The use of AI to guide the group interviews helped the evaluators

- Understand the complex organizational context of the World Bank, which is a large, decentralized international organization of about 10,000, of which 3,000 work in 109 country offices and 1,000 are traveling at any given time. Storytelling about successful instances and the structured interaction of AI enabled the evaluators to build trust with the participants quickly in order to explore important contextual factors.

*(Continued)*

---

(Continued)

- Mine the knowledge experiences of WB ISG staff who come in contact regularly with operations staff. Operations staff are hard to reach, so ISG staff stationed in divisions across the WB were able to check with operations staff and to share useful information about their understanding of operations' staff needs.

- Understand the "languages" of the World Bank staff who use specific terminology related to their technology and international development project work. For outside consultants who have limited time to establish a productive working relationship with the staff, this can be quite a challenge. The structured story-telling of the AI interviews bridged this gap, and enabled the evaluators to gain insights beyond the typical complaints about annoying technical issues, such as passwords and favorite fonts.

- Use the focus group interview results to develop an online survey that was sent to a sample of the Operations staff.

In this example, the full Appreciative Inquiry process was used to conduct the individual and group interviews. The evaluators believe that using the AI process was an effective complement to the other data collection methods used in this multifaceted evaluation project.

---

# Designing and Conducting Surveys Using Appreciative Questions

Not surprisingly, surveys are the most often used data collection method, and usually consist of a predetermined set of questions that are distributed by mail, fax, email, or handed to individuals. Though surveys are usually self-administered, they can also be read to respondents. (For more information on designing surveys, see Bradburn, Sudman, & Wansink, 2004; Czaja & Blair, 2005; Dillman, 1999; Fink, 2003; Fowler, 2002.) Using surveys to collect evaluation data has several advantages. These include

- Administration is comparatively inexpensive and easy even when gathering data from large numbers of people spread over wide geographic areas.

- The same questions are presented in the same manner to all respondents, with no interpretation on the part of the evaluator, thus reducing the chance of evaluator bias.

- Many people, particularly from the United States and western European countries, are familiar with surveys.

- Some respondents may feel more comfortable responding to a survey than participating in an interview.

- Tabulation of closed-ended responses is an easy and straightforward process.

- The use of surveys may increase the likelihood of obtaining a representative sample. (Russ-Eft & Preskill, 2001, p. 227)

As is true for designing interview guides, a survey might include a few appreciative questions, or it could be made up entirely of appreciative questions. And, as with designing interview guides, the extent to which Appreciative Inquiry is applied depends on the requirements of the evaluation, the topic, and the client's comfort level and experience with AI. Two types of appreciative questions can be developed for a survey: (1) open-ended questions and (2) closed questions that ask participants to select from a pre-determined list of options.

### Open-Ended Appreciative Survey Questions

Including open-ended questions that ask respondents to describe their peak experiences, values, and wishes (*Inquire*) poses an interesting dilemma for evaluators who wish to use a survey as a data collection method. Asking survey respondents to tell their story of a peak or successful experience requires that they spend a significant amount of time thinking about it and writing their response. Yet, many will choose not to respond either because they do not believe they have the time, or they are uncomfortable with their writing ability (Czaja & Blair, 2005; Edwards, Thomas, Rosenfeld, & Booth-Kewley, 1997). Even if respondents are willing to tell their story in writing, they do not benefit from an attentive listener who also provides important nonverbal feedback, as occurs in the appreciative interview process. These issues can be somewhat minimized if the survey is completed online and/or is implemented synchronously over the Internet or Intranet with an interviewer. The following example illustrates how this has been done in an evaluation.

---

**Case Study 10**

#### Using a Survey at the Maui High Performance Computing Center[5]

An example of a survey that included open-ended appreciative questions is one that was used by the Maui High Performance Computing Center (MHPCC), titled "Appreciative Inquiry Organizational Survey." It was sent to employees via the organization's Intranet in an attempt to obtain members' stories about their experiences working for the MHPCC. The survey included the following questions:

*(Continued)*

(Continued)

Starting back at the time you began working at the MHPCC . . .

- What first attracted you to the MHPCC?
- What were your initial impressions when you joined?
- How have your impressions changed since then?
- What keeps you here?

In your work here, you have probably experienced ups and downs, some high points and low points. Think about a time that stands out to you as a high point—a time when you felt most involved, most effective, most engaged. It might have been recently or some time ago.

- What was going on?
- Who were the significant people involved?
- What were the most important factors in the MHPCC that helped to make it a high-point experience (e.g., leadership qualities, rewards, structure, relationships, skills, etc.)?
- What was especially important/memorable about this one experience for you?

*(Continued below)*

Asking an open-ended *values* question on a survey may also be challenging when people are asked to respond in writing and without the interaction of others. The importance of a *values* question when used in interviews is that it grounds the respondent's story in his or her personal values. When participants share these values, it highlights their various definitions of success and their wishes for the future. Surveys, however, lack the dynamic created by the interaction between the interviewee and the interviewer, which emphasizes the importance of honoring the interviewees' experiences. Yet, if the survey is delivered over the Internet or Intranet, as in the case of the Maui High Performance Computing Center, asking *values* questions may produce insightful results.

(Continued)

The following are the MHPCC survey questions regarding organization members' values:

Think about the nature of your work at the MHPCC.

- What aspect of your work do you value most (i.e., most interesting, most meaningful, most satisfying)?
- Describe one outstanding or successful achievement or contribution of which you are particularly proud.
- What made it outstanding?
- What unique skills or qualities did you draw on to achieve this result?
- What organizational factors helped to create or support your achievement?
- What is the single most important thing the MHPCC has contributed to your life, professionally and/or personally?

*(Continued on page 93)*

Even if it is not desirable or feasible to ask open-ended *story* and *values* questions on a survey (particularly a written survey), it is possible to include an open-ended *wishes* question, especially at the end of a survey. Such a question might be phrased, "What three wishes do you have that would help make this program or organization consistently perform at its very best?" Since most respondents are likely to have ideas for how a program or organization could be strengthened based on their experiences, this question may elicit informative and useful data that would not require a great deal of writing.

---

(Continued)

Continuing with the MHPCC example, their survey included the following *wishes* questions:

As an organization, there are many changes we can make now and in the future to improve and evolve with the times. However, there are some core strengths, values, and ways of working that we should continue and keep doing, even as we change in the future.

- What are three things we do best that you would like to see the MHPCC keep or continue doing—even as things change in the future?
- What three wishes would you make to heighten the vitality and health of the MHPCC?
- What part could you, do you want to play in making these wishes materialize?

---

As this example illustrates, it might be necessary to ask several questions related to each aspect of AI's *Inquire* phase for respondents to fully articulate what would normally be asked in a few questions during an interview.

---

**Case Study 11**

## Using a Web-Based Survey to Evaluate a Graduate School Program[6]

In this evaluation, the evaluators developed and implemented a Web-based survey using open-ended appreciative questions with 72 current and former students. The evaluation team (eight students and two faculty members) was particularly interested in determining how well the program was working and how the program's offerings could be improved. The five-item survey consisted of an introductory question:

1. Why did you choose this program?

A *story* question:

2. Share a highlight of your time so far in the TTD Program. As you share your story, consider the following: What made it a high point? Who was involved?

*(Continued)*

(Continued)

What did they do that made it a good experience? What did you do that made it a good experience?

A *values* question:

3. Based on your experience so far, what do you value most about the program? What would you define as core characteristics of the program (without these, the division and program would not be what it is)? Please be specific.

A *wishes* question:

4. If you were the "student-in-charge" of this program and could have three wishes for the program granted, what would you wish? How would the program be different if your three wishes were incorporated into the curriculum?

And a question concerning students' experiences with using distance technologies:

5. Many of the courses are delivered partially or fully using distance technologies such as WebCT and interactive video. What is it like to be in such a class? What courses have you had that are actually (or you believe would be) better delivered in a distance format? What role do you believe distance technologies should play in the future of the Program?

Forty-four of the 72 (61%) students responded to the survey. The evaluation team analyzed the data and developed a set of recommendations based on the evaluation findings. One month after receiving the report, the faculty met to develop an action plan for implementing the evaluation's recommendations. They believe that, "While serious issues surfaced and were addressed, valuable information, key insights, and pleasant surprises made this an evaluation report that was acted upon rather than relegated to a bookshelf to collect dust" (Norum, Wells, Hoadley, Geary, & Thompson, 2004, p. 207). At the same time, the evaluation team knew that some might think the faculty only wanted to hear about the positive aspects of the program, but found, "as students described their wishes for the future of the Program, problems and criticisms surfaced. However, because the focus was on what was going right, it was easier to turn those problems and criticism into positive recommendations" (Norum et al., 2004, p. 199), which included areas in need of improvement.

It is important to remember that in cases where stories of peak experiences and values questions are not asked, responses to a wishes question will not be grounded in the study of success. Rather, they will reflect whatever is on the mind of the respondent at that time. Finally, when any kind of open-ended question is included on a survey, it is critical to consider the characteristics of potential respondents. Their reading and writing ability, their access to the Internet (if appropriate), and the likelihood of their responding to open-ended questions should all be considered prior to designing a survey using open-ended appreciative questions.

## Closed-Ended Appreciative Survey Questions

Closed-ended survey questions typically ask participants to rate or rank some aspect of what is being evaluated, with the most commonly used format being the four- to seven-point Likert scale. It is possible, however, to obtain more useful information from a closed-ended survey item by reframing it to be appreciatively oriented. The following is an example of a closed-ended questionnaire that was used as part of a larger evaluation effort.

---

**Case Study 12**

### Using a Survey to Evaluate the African Women's Media Center[7]

In an evaluation of the African Women's Media Center (AWMC), Catsambas and Webb (2000; also see Catsambas & Webb, 2003) designed and developed an appreciative questionnaire, which was translated into French for Francophone members, and distributed it to all members via mail, email and/or fax, as well as posted on the Internet, and were reflective of the themes and visions identified in the AI session conducted with the AWMC advisory committee. The questionnaire (see Figure 4.1) was mailed to 650 people throughout Africa and was posted on the organization's Web site.

The specific sequencing of the appreciative questions asked respondents to reflect on their own participation in the organization, the contributions it had made to them as members, the contributions and future directions they imagined, and the investments they were willing to make to build that future. The questionnaire worked well in the context of the broader evaluation methodology and furthered the dialogue that had started through the individual and group interviews conducted earlier.

---

## Summary

This chapter distinguished between asking positive and appreciative questions, emphasizing that reframing questions appreciatively generates more useful and valuable information for an evaluation. It also illustrated how non-AI questions can be reframed to be more appreciative—that is, to focus on stories of peak experiences and on participants' values and wishes relative to what is being evaluated. An interview guide or survey may include only one appreciative question, or it can consist entirely of appreciative questions, and it may be designed from scratch, or appreciative questions can be added to an already developed interview guide or survey. While AI can be adapted to conducting individual interviews, it is most effective when the evaluator can implement paired interviews, or a least a group interview where participants can hear each other's stories. This is especially significant relative to designing appreciative questions for surveys. High-quality and useful data can be obtained from appreciative questions posed on surveys, but the evaluator needs to keep in mind that respondents are less likely to provide lengthy written responses, and will not have the benefit of hearing other respondent's stories of success, values, wishes, and visions. Nevertheless, regardless of whatever constraints or conditions evaluators find themselves in, even asking one appreciative question on an interview guide or survey can provide data rich with insights while simultaneously initiating a process of positive improvement and change.

## Notes

1. Provided by Tamara Walser, Windwalker Corporation, McLean, Virginia. This case is an evaluation of the National Assessment of Educational Progress (NAEP) State Service Center. Reprinted with permission.

2. The evaluation was conducted by University Research Co., LLC, Bethesda, MD. Reprinted with permission.

3. This case example was provided by Dawn Smart, Clegg & Associates, Seattle, WA. Reprinted with permission.

4. The evaluation was conducted by EnCompass LLC, Potomac, MD. Reprinted with permission.

5. This survey was retrieved from http://www.orgdct.com/maui_high_performance_computing_.htm on April 15, 2005. Reprinted with permission.

6. This example describes an evaluation of the graduate program in Technology for Training and Development (TDD) at the University of South Dakota that was conducted by Norum, Wells, Hoadley, Geary, and Thompson (2004). Reprinted with permission.

7. Implemented by EnCompass LLC, Potomac, Maryland. Reprinted with permission.

MEETING YOUR NEEDS:

# AN AWMC QUESTIONNAIRE

The AWMC is asking for your help in evaluating the programs and resources it has offered over the last three years for African women journalists. We are also asking for your advice in planning future activities. Your participation in this survey will give the AWMC insight to ensure its programs address the issues you believe are most important and in a way that best serves your interests. We hope you will take just a few minutes to respond to the questionnaire and send it back to us **by July 30, 2000** by fax at: 202-496-1977; or you can answer the questionnaire directly on the AWMC web site at www.awmc.com. We thank you in advance for helping us to create AWMC programs and materials that will strengthen women's voices in the news media. To thank you, we will send you selected **copies of AWMC materials** if we receive your answer by our deadline, July 30th.

1. I live in _____
   *(fill in country)* and I am
   ❑ Female   ❑ Male

2. I work in
   ❑ Print media, e.g., newspaper
   ❑ Television
   ❑ Radio
   ❑ Other _____

3. My position is
   ❑ Reporter
   ❑ Manager/Editor
   ❑ Other _____

4. I have worked in media for
   ❑ less than 2 years      ❑ 2-5 years
   ❑ 6-10 years             ❑ more than 10 years

5. My best experience(s) with the AWMC have been in the area(s) of *(mark as many as apply)*
   ❑ Skills training
   ❑ Using the Web site
   ❑ On the Wire (newsletter)
   ❑ The cyber conference
   ❑ Carole Simpson Leadership Institute
   ❑ Handbook for Media Leadership
   ❑ Resource Directory for Women Journalists
   ❑ Networking
   ❑ Other _____

6. The most important aspects of the AWMC for me are *(mark as many as apply)*
   ❑ Training
   ❑ Networking/support systems
   ❑ Increasing visibility for women
   ❑ Creating opportunities for women
   ❑ Recognizing women's talents
   ❑ Seeking women's opinions
   ❑ Data bank as a resource
   ❑ Empowerment/confidence
   ❑ Other _____

7. For me, the most important topics for training that the AWMC should offer are:
   ❑ General journalism skills training
   ❑ Negotiating skills training
   ❑ Broadcasting production skills
   ❑ Internet use and research skills
   ❑ Leadership training
   ❑ Gender sensitivity
   ❑ Political and elections reporting
   ❑ Business/economics reporting
   ❑ HIV/AIDS reporting
   ❑ Management training
   ❑ Other _____

8. I mostly communicate with the AWMC through
   ❑ The AWMC Newsletter
   ❑ The AWMC Web site
   ❑ AWMC programs
   ❑ Telephone/fax
   ❑ My women's media association
   ❑ Other AWMC members
   ❑ E-mail
   ❑ Other _____

9. The best aspects of AWMC programs and events are *(mark as many as apply)*
   ❑ AWMC programs are organized well and run smoothly
   ❑ The topics covered are critical for African women in media
   ❑ The wonderful and inspiring stories from other women
   ❑ Meeting people who became important in my life and work
   ❑ I learned new skills
   ❑ I learned about reporting on current issues
   ❑ I became aware of useful resources
   ❑ I became connected to other women in media
   ❑ I gained respect and stature in my work
   ❑ I received reinforcement of my power through exposure to other women leaders
   ❑ Other _____

10. If I had the opportunity, I would like to get more involved in AWMC activities in *(mark all that apply)*
   ❑ Attending training programs
   ❑ Networking, promoting women journalists in my own country, and helping to strengthen my own country's media association
   ❑ Helping design and organize programs
   ❑ Helping to find additional funds for the AWMC
   ❑ Contributing to the newsletter
   ❑ I love AWMC activities, but cannot devote time to the organization right now
   ❑ I don't find the AWMC's work directly relevant to my work and issues
   ❑ Mentoring other women journalists on the Continent
   ❑ Serving as a trainer for an AWMC program

11. Mark the statement that best represents your view
   ❑ The AWMC is unique in what it contributes to women in media in Africa and worldwide
   ❑ Although it is not unique, the AWMC makes important contributions to women in media in Africa and worldwide
   ❑ Although the AWMC make important contributions to women in media in Africa and worldwide, I have found my issues and concerns addressed best at
   _____
   _____
   *(fill in which organization)*

**Figure 4.1**     An AWMC Questionnaire                                    *(Continued)*

**Figure 4.1** (Continued)

12. The African Women's Media Center is working to address many issues important to African women in media. Please indicated which of the issues listed below you believe the AWMC is <u>currently addressing</u>, and which issues the AWMC <u>should address</u> in the future by ticking the appropriate boxes on the right *(mark as many as apply).* Then, please mark on the left column entitled "Rank" the <u>Top Five</u> issues that the AWMC should address in the future.

| RANK | ASPECT/GOAL | AWMC addresses now | AWMC should address in the future |
|---|---|---|---|
| | **INCREASING VISIBILITY FOR WOMEN** | | |
| | Recognize achievements of women and increase their visibility in the news media | ❏ | ❏ |
| | Help make women's issues and perspectives more "mainstream"—seek women experts, get women's stories, highlight gender issues | ❏ | ❏ |
| | **EMPOWERMENT/CONFIDENCE BUILDING** | | |
| | Develop strategies and information on fighting discrimination and sexual harassment | ❏ | ❏ |
| | Address issues of cultural norms and religious taboos for professional women | ❏ | ❏ |
| | Encourage women in traditional male areas of journalism—e.g., economics, foreign policy, science, politics, business | ❏ | ❏ |
| | Offer ideas and experience for balancing work and family life | ❏ | ❏ |
| | Help promote women in management and leadership positions | ❏ | ❏ |
| | **NETWORKING/SUPPORT SYSTEMS** | | |
| | Facilitate networking among women journalists | ❏ | ❏ |
| | Offer role models for women | ❏ | ❏ |
| | Involve men in media in dialogue about women in media | ❏ | ❏ |
| | **TRAINING** | | |
| | Create opportunities for skills training | ❏ | ❏ |
| | Create opportunities for training using the Internet | ❏ | ❏ |
| | **RESOURCES** | | |
| | Develop and communicate strategies for establishing alternative media | ❏ | ❏ |
| | Support freedom of the press—publicize issues of persecution, risks to journalists | ❏ | ❏ |
| | Strengthen women's media associations | ❏ | ❏ |
| | Promote democracy | ❏ | ❏ |
| | Develop awards programs (local, Africa-wide) | ❏ | ❏ |
| | Provide information on exchange programs | ❏ | ❏ |
| | Other: | ❏ | ❏ |
| | Other: | ❏ | ❏ |

13. I also wish to receive the following AWMC resources *(click as many as apply)*:
   ❏ AWMC Resource Directory
   ❏ AWMC Leadership Handbook

Please update your contact information for our database: _____

_____

*(fill in name and address)*

**AWMC: B.P. 21186 Dakar-Ponty, Dakar, Senegal**

Tel: 221.823.9965 or 823.8687 • Fax: 221.822.4164 or 823.0157 • Email: awmc@metissacana.sn

Source: AWMC. Reprinted with permission.

# Using Appreciative Inquiry to Develop Evaluation Systems 5

*Vision without action is merely a dream. Action without vision just passes the time. Vision with action can change the world!*

—Joel Arthur Barker

This chapter addresses the third use of Appreciative Inquiry within an evaluation context—using AI to develop evaluation systems. As a whole-systems approach, AI helps align evaluation activities with an organization's mission and performance goals. All too often, evaluations are conducted as intermittent, standalone, disconnected studies. This chapter first discusses the need for evaluation systems and what elements make up such systems. It then explains how Appreciative Inquiry can be used to design evaluation systems and provides two cases as illustrative examples.

As our world has become increasingly interconnected and the pace of change has quickened, organizations have employed a variety of strategies to develop ways of detecting, understanding, and adapting to shifting internal and external requirements. These include

- Investing in monitoring and evaluation activities in order to assess and support continuous progress, to provide ongoing feedback to leaders and funders, and to learn from the experiences of organization members

- Developing knowledge management systems and increasing technology access and connectivity

- Providing learning opportunities using blended methods of classroom training, eLearning, mentoring, and communities of practice
- Strengthening leadership capacity through programs that develop organization members' emotional intelligence
- Aligning organizational structures and processes to adapt to evolving goals and customer needs and expectations

Within this context, Appreciative Inquiry has much to offer organizations as they strive to remain relevant, competitive, creative, and socially responsible. In particular, AI has a unique role to play in supporting an organization's efforts to build and sustain evaluation systems. As organizations continue to build their internal evaluation capacity and become committed to ongoing and embedded evaluation practice, it becomes ever more critical that they develop evaluation systems that organize, guide, and communicate their work. At an *organizational level,* designing and implementing an evaluation system ensures that all evaluation activities contribute to continuous learning, informed decision making, and the use of evaluation findings. Such a system also reinforces the likelihood that

- Evaluation activities relate to and contribute to the organization's strategic plan, vision, and mission
- Evaluation results are fed into decision-making systems and structures
- Evaluation activities are integrated and connected and, as a result, maximize resources
- Organization members learn from each evaluation experience and share that learning

At the *individual and group levels,* the development of an evaluation system helps organization members understand how

- Evaluation affects all programs and processes in the organization
- Different parts of the evaluation system work together
- The findings of one evaluation may influence the design and implementation of future evaluations
- Evaluation is everyone's responsibility
- Evaluation is integral to operational management and decision making

Ultimately, the establishment of an evaluation system communicates an organization's long-term commitment to inquiry as a means of achieving its goals and objectives. This chapter describes how Appreciative Inquiry can be used to help organizations develop evaluation systems regardless of how much experience they have had with evaluation.

# Designing an Evaluation System

Simply stated, a system is "a set of components that work together for the overall objective of the whole" (Haines, 2000, p. vi). Thus, an evaluation system is a means for identifying, developing, implementing, and sustaining those things that support evaluative inquiry. What follows in this chapter is an example of an evaluation system that has grown out of our evaluation work with numerous U.S. and international public, nonprofit, corporate, government, education, and healthcare organizations.[1] In our view, an evaluation system is made up of five essential components (see Figure 5.1).

1. Leadership Commitment

2. Evaluation Vision and Philosophy

3. Evaluation Strategic Plan

4. Evaluation Design and Implementation Requirements
   - Evaluation Plans
   - Technology Resources and Infrastructure
   - Communication Systems
   - Flexible and Responsive Evaluation Practices

5. Personnel and Financial Resources

**Figure 5.1**     Components of an Evaluation System

When each component is fully designed and implemented, the evaluation system should work efficiently and effectively—it should provide useful, timely, and cost-effective evaluation results. If, for any reason, the organization chooses not to include one or more of the system's components, it is important to understand that the overall system's effectiveness will likely be compromised. That is, each of the system's elements is related and is interdependent with the others; a change in (or exclusion of) one component will ultimately affect the quality and impact of the remaining components—that is, the evaluation process and its outcomes.

## System Component 1: Leadership Commitment

Successful evaluation practice is highly dependent on how effective leaders (at all levels within the organization) are at communicating the belief that evaluation is a meaningful and important activity, and that evaluation is about building on the organization's strengths as well as identifying areas for improvement. Thus, leaders must consistently communicate the importance of evaluation for decision making, and encourage a culture of inquiry based on asking questions, reflection, and dialogue. Leaders who support evaluation

- Provide resources (financial, time, personnel) for conducting quality evaluations
- Demonstrate the value of evaluation by using evaluation findings to make decisions
- Encourage organization members to participate in evaluations and use their findings
- Use evaluation findings to make improvements to the organization's programs, processes, policies, products, and systems
- Use evaluation findings to share lessons learned
- Celebrate and communicate an evaluation's findings and how those relate to the future of the organization
- Frame negative findings as opportunities to improve, learn, and grow

Because organization members are acutely attuned to the actions of its leaders, they know when the organization is sincerely committed to an effort, and when it is not. In other words, the organization's leadership must walk the talk of evaluative inquiry every day. Leaders must be champions of evaluation—they should be able to recognize good evaluation practice, they should model data-based decision making, and they should expect that all members will engage in evaluative inquiry as part of their jobs.

### System Component 2: Evaluation Vision and Philosophy

Having a clear articulation of the organization's vision and philosophy about evaluation and its role in the organization is critical for supporting ongoing evaluation work. This information not only helps guide the system's development, but it also educates members about the value of evaluation and the nature of a successful evaluation system.

A vision statement for evaluation describes the organization's values and beliefs regarding evaluation practice. It communicates the role that evaluation plays in organizational decision making, why evaluation is important, and how evaluation contributes to the future of the organization. The vision statement should be communicated throughout the organization in a variety of formats and should form the basis for all evaluation work. Once the vision statement has been developed, it should be revisited annually to determine if any changes are warranted.

Related to the vision statement is a statement of evaluation philosophy. This statement communicates the organization's preferred model or approach (not methods or design) that will guide evaluation practice. It is important to communicate the organization's evaluation philosophy in a number of ways so that all members understand the purpose of evaluation and its role in the organization. For example, the evaluation philosophy statement could be communicated through

- An email message to organization members prior to the beginning of any evaluation
- Posters or flyers displayed throughout the organization
- An evaluation column in the organization's internal newsletter
- Verbal statements made at staff meetings or other opportune times
- A footnote in every evaluation report
- Brochures that are used to market various programs and services

The following illustrates one organization's evaluation vision and philosophy:

*We are deeply committed to using a collaborative, participatory, and learning oriented approach to evaluation. Evaluation is often most successful when it is conducted by teams of organization members (perhaps including external constituents) who have different experiences and responsibilities relative to the program or service being evaluated. Working collaboratively on an evaluation enables employees to*

- *Pool their collective knowledge and skills regarding the program being evaluated as well as the practice of evaluation*
- *Make public particular biases that can be acknowledged, and managed*
- *Build their evaluation capacity*
- *Increase the credibility and quality of the evaluation*
- *Share their learning about the evaluand and evaluation with others in the organization*
- *Appreciate the work of others in the organization*
- *Develop new insights into their work and the work of the organization*
- *Complete the evaluation in a more timely and cost effective way*

An evaluation philosophy statement could also convey the organization's beliefs about the use of evaluation findings and its commitment to the ethical and professional conduct of evaluation by grounding all evaluation activities in the *Program Evaluation Standards* and the American Evaluation Association's (AEA) *Guiding Principles* (see www.eval.org for more information). The following statement reflects this promise:

*We are dedicated to conducting quality and useful evaluations and believe that both internal and external evaluators must act ethically and professionally. Therefore, evaluation practice should, at all times, reflect the standards and principles of the evaluation profession. When questions arise concerning the "right thing to do," these standards and principles should be consulted.*

An organization that wishes to ground its evaluation philosophy in Appreciative Inquiry might also include the following statement:

*Evaluations conducted in this organization will ensure the study of successful practices and the alignment of evaluation with the vision of the organization. Whenever appropriate and feasible, appreciative questions will be included on surveys and interview guides when implemented for evaluation purposes.*

Regardless of how the statement is worded, the power and influence of having an evaluation vision and philosophy statement made explicit and public cannot be overestimated.

## System Component 3: Evaluation Strategic Plan

An evaluation strategic plan describes how, when, by whom, and to what extent various programs, processes, products, policies, and services will be evaluated. Decisions regarding when to evaluate may depend on various factors including (a) the length of time the program has been in operation, (b) how the findings will be used—what kinds of decisions need to be made, and (c) how often the program is offered. Having an evaluation strategic plan ensures that

- Organization members integrate evaluation into their day-to-day work
- There are sufficient resources for evaluation activities
- There is little to no duplication of evaluation efforts
- Important aspects of the program or organization are periodically evaluated
- There is some degree of coordination and collaboration between and among various evaluation efforts
- There may be learning across evaluation teams.
- There is responsible use of resources

An evaluation strategic plan is an excellent tool for communicating the ongoing progress and outcomes of various programs and processes within the organization. As a result, the information gathered from evaluations may also provide invaluable feedback for reviewing and revising the organization's strategic plan.

## System Component 4: Evaluation Design and Implementation Requirements

To ensure that the evaluation system is implemented in ways that reflect professional evaluation practice, it should include guidelines for designing and implementing credible and useful evaluations. The following describes four requirements that contribute to successful evaluations.

### Evaluation Plans

For every evaluation conducted, regardless of its scope and cost, an evaluation plan should be developed. As described in Chapters 2 and 3, an evaluation plan, at the very least, communicates the evaluation's purpose, key questions, stakeholders, design, data collection and analysis methods, timeline, budget, and other project management information. The evaluation plan is a means for establishing the evaluation team's role and responsibilities, and for communicating with others the purpose of the evaluation and the intended uses of the evaluation's results. Included in the evaluation plan should be a logic model of the program being evaluated.

### Technology Resources and Infrastructure

In the last several years, technology has been playing an increasingly important role in the design and implementation of evaluation studies. For example, evaluators are

- Using concept mapping tools for developing evaluation logic models
- Using groupware to conduct interviews
- Designing and implementing online surveys
- Conducting interviews over the Internet or Intranet
- Using voice-recognition software for transcribing interviews
- Using qualitative analysis software packages
- Using quantitative analysis software packages
- Using the organization's Intranet or the Internet to store and distribute evaluation findings

- Developing knowledge management systems in which evaluation processes and findings are stored
- Using project management software to track evaluation activities
- Discussing evaluation findings and recommendations for action in online chat rooms

In order to fully maximize the use of technology in evaluation practice, it is essential that the evaluation system incorporate guidelines for developing a technology infrastructure that (a) supports the purchase of computer hardware, peripherals, and software, (b) establishes and maintains network accessibility, and (c) supports the hiring of individuals who can develop and sustain the use of various technologies. A review of the organization's larger technology infrastructure may also provide ideas for how evaluation activities may tap into the organization's existing databases.

## Communication Systems

An evaluation system should include the means for communicating and reporting an evaluation's progress and results. Not only should those involved in conducting the evaluation be apprised of the evaluation's findings and recommendations, but the stakeholders should also be provided with some form of communication that summarizes the evaluation's purpose, key questions, design, and results. If the organization wants to build the evaluation capacity of its members, then it must commit to sharing what is being learned from its evaluation work. In addition to the typical lengthy final report, there are many ways in which evaluation processes and findings can be communicated and reported. These include executive summaries, newsletters, posters, flyers, email messages, written memos, verbal presentations, Web pages, press release, video/DVD, and working sessions. (For more strategies on communicating and reporting, see Torres, Preskill, & Piontek, 2005.)

## Flexible and Responsive Evaluation Practices

Because all evaluation contexts and conditions are different, evaluation practice should not reflect a "one size fits all" approach, nor should it be rigid in its design and implementation. Rather, evaluation needs to be both flexible and responsive to organizations when they experience things such as (a) unanticipated organizational changes (e.g., change in leadership, mergers, lay-offs, closings), (b) federal and state regulations and requirements, and (c) political agendas and pressures. Many evaluators have been called on to change an evaluation question, to redesign the data collection plan, or to work with a new stakeholder, all as a result of unanticipated changes in the organization. In terms of developing an evaluation system, being flexible and responsive means designing each evaluation according to the stakeholders' needs for information, choosing an evaluation design and data collection methods that will credibly answer the key questions, and taking care to perform evaluation in accordance with the profession's code of ethics and values. This ultimately involves understanding a range of evaluation models, approaches, and techniques (see Chapter 2 for a list of evaluator competencies).

### System Component 5:
### Personnel and Financial Resources

Evaluation systems will only succeed in serving the organization if there are adequate resources dedicated to designing and conducting quality evaluations. In terms of personnel, this translates into having enough people to implement evaluations as called for in the evaluation strategic plan and provide for hiring outside consultants to train and facilitate certain evaluation-related tasks of the evaluation if necessary. If the goal is to build the capacity of organization members to conduct evaluations, then employees should also be encouraged to participate in evaluation-related studies, workshops, and university courses. (For more information on evaluation workshops and courses, see American Evaluation Association, www.eval.org; The Evaluator's Institute, www.evaluatorsinstitute.com; and Claremont Graduate University, www.cgu.edu/sbos. An evaluation system also requires the allocation of financial resources so that employees may conduct quality and timely evaluations. These resources may result in hiring more internal staff; reallocating work loads; purchasing software and other technologies; paying for travel, materials, telephone, and duplicating; and hiring external consultants. This might mean establishing a line item for evaluation in every department's budget.

# Developing an Evaluation System
# Using Appreciative Inquiry

The process of developing an evaluation system is inherently a strategic planning process applied to evaluation. Using Appreciative Inquiry in this context is particularly valuable because it

- Enables organizations to build on their success, create visions, think innovatively, and develop bold plans for achieving those visions

- Clarifies desired outcomes from evaluation practice

- Identifies organization members' values concerning the role of evaluation in the organization

- Clarifies the relationship between evaluation, learning, and decision making, and how the program or organization can benefit from such inquiry

- Is a whole-system process that facilitates the inclusion of many stakeholders

Because of Appreciative Inquiry's flexibility, it can be applied in various ways to develop any or all of the evaluation system's components. Using AI for this purpose is most effective when large numbers of stakeholders are involved, and the organization's leaders are fully engaged in the process. The extent to which, and how much, AI is used to develop each component of the evaluation system may depend on how much time is available and the organization's experience with evaluation. For example, the process may differ depending on whether organization members have significant experience using evaluation in the conduct of their work, or whether it is a new activity that is being added to their current work processes and job requirements. If the organization already has experience with evaluation and wants to develop an evaluation system, the topic of the AI would be *evaluation*. Since organization members have evaluation experiences from which they can discuss peak experiences, the information they provide can form a solid foundation for developing the new evaluation system.

On the other hand, if organization members have little experience with evaluation, focusing the AI on *evaluation* might not produce useful or relevant information for developing an evaluation system. In this case, the evaluator might be more successful by first focusing the AI on organization members' *exceptional experiences related to the work of the program or organization*. Following the paired interviews and sharing of stories, participants could then consider how evaluation might support the themes that emerged from their reflections on peak work experiences (*Inquire*). This discussion would likely result in a vision of what constitutes meaningful evaluation practice (*Imagine*). Figure 5.2 outlines these two strategies for developing an evaluation system in organizations with differing levels of evaluation experience.

The major difference between these two approaches is the focus of the inquiry. For organizations that have little to no evaluation experience, the AI process helps them articulate their views of excellence for the organization overall. Once participants are grounded in stories of success, it is easier to move them toward focusing on how an evaluation system would further contribute to the organization's effectiveness.

| Organization Has Evaluation Experience | Organization Has Little or No Evaluation Experience |
|---|---|
| • AI process focused on peak experiences with *evaluation* (*Inquire*)<br><br>• Themes of exceptional evaluation (*Inquire*)<br><br>• Vision of evaluation for the organization (*Imagine*)<br><br>• Provocative propositions translating the vision of excellent evaluation into the various parts of the organizational system and processes (*Innovate*)<br><br>• Draft of the proposed evaluation system developed by the evaluation team<br><br>• Development of evaluation system components | • AI process focused on peak experiences in organizational *performance* (*Inquire*)<br><br>• Themes of exceptional organizational performance (*Inquire*)<br><br>• Vision of excellence in the organization (*Imagine*)<br><br>• Brainstorming and affinity analysis of desired outcomes in the organization<br><br>• Discussion of how evaluation can support the desired outcomes (helping the organization to learn, support decision making, promote knowledge sharing)<br><br>• Vision and values for evaluation (*Imagine*)<br><br>• Draft of possible evaluation system options by the evaluation team |

**Figure 5.2**   Options for Using Appreciative Inquiry to Develop an Evaluation System

## Examples of Using Appreciative Inquiry to Develop an Evaluation System

The two case examples that follow illustrate each of these organizational contexts. In the first case, Sandia National Laboratories had significant experience in conducting evaluations of their training and organization development efforts, but they lacked an integrated approach that was cost effective and user-friendly. In the second case, which highlights the World Bank's Conflict Resolution system, the organization had little evaluation experience. This case describes how a newly emerged system of five offices had just developed a strategic plan and had participated in the annual staff survey. Although one office had some experience using exit surveys, as a whole, the group had not designed or conducted any evaluations. Each of these case examples illustrates how Appreciative Inquiry was used to develop their respective evaluation systems.

## Building an Evaluation System for Sandia National Laboratories' Corporate Education, Development, and Training Department[2]

The mission of the Corporate Education, Development, and Training (CEDT) Department at Sandia National Laboratories (SNL) is "Leading the creation and implementation of a full range of results-oriented development and training solutions that contribute to Sandia's mission success. Our competent innovative experts partner with customers to excel in a complex business environment." Toward those ends, CEDT offers an extensive array of learning opportunities delivered through instructor-led classroom training, Web-based and computer courses, self-study, coaching, mentoring, and consulting on a wide variety of topics.

The organization's programs and services were primarily evaluated through pre- and post-class assessments and post-course reaction surveys. With the large number of courses offered, CEDT employees have found it difficult to identify exactly how data are collected throughout the organization and how to systematically collect valid and usable data that reflect the effectiveness of their programs and services. In addition, employees have not been able to "roll up" data across types of delivery systems and report information regarding their effectiveness to all organization members.

In order for the CEDT Department to develop an evaluation system that provides valid, useful, and ongoing evaluation information, the evaluators were contracted to conduct a needs analysis of the existing evaluation deployment of CEDT and non-CEDT courses. The product was to be a user-friendly report that included (a) a framework for a comprehensive evaluation system, (b) a review of their current evaluation process strengths and weaknesses, (c) suggestions for possible software tools and techniques to collect online data, and (d) a set of recommendations for improving the current evaluation processes and system.

During a 7-hour meeting, 43 of the Department's 52 employees (83%) participated in an Appreciative Inquiry process. Participants were told that based on their previous evaluation experiences they would be asked to provide information that would be used to develop an evaluation framework and system.

Beginning with the *Inquire* phase, participants, in pairs, interviewed each other for ten minutes (each). They were asked to consider the following:

> Think of a time when you knew that a CEDT evaluation process was working well. You were confident and excited that important and useful data were being collected and you felt energized about the evaluation process. What was happening? Who did it involve? What made this evaluation process (or outcome) so successful? Why was it successful? What was your role? What value did you add to this evaluation process?

After 20 minutes, the pairs were asked to join two other pairs to form a group of six. In this group they were to tell the highlights of their partner's story (2 minutes each), and then to look for themes across the group's stories. As the themes emerged, they wrote them on flip-chart paper (an easel with paper was placed at each table). Each group was then asked to share its themes with the larger group. The following is a sample of its responses to the questions that asked them to reflect on the aspects of the evaluation process that were working well and what made the process so successful.

- We analyze data
- Use data for improvement, decision making
- Ability to summarize data
- Evaluation was specific to what was evaluated (course or program)
- Immediate feedback to instructor(s), course manager, participants
- Information beyond test scores/performance tests
- All course evaluations measure against SNL competencies, which are incorporated into course objectives
- Multiple means/venues of data collection
- Funded enough $$ to conduct evaluation
- Customer involvement/buy-in/funding
- Resulting data/findings are trustworthy, useful, and *used*

After a brief discussion about the similarities and differences between the groups (there were many commonalities among the lists), the *Imagine* phase of the AI process was initiated. Participants were asked to work with their groups of six and to discuss the following question (30 minutes). They were also instructed to write the themes of their group's visions on flip-chart paper.

Imagine that you have been asleep for 5 years, and when you awake, you look around and see that the CEDT Department has developed a comprehensive, effective, and efficient evaluation system. This system provides timely and useful information for decision making and action relative to the programs and services the Department provides in the areas of education, development, and training. The evaluation system has been so successful that the United States Secretary of Energy has announced that the CEDT Department will be receiving an award for outstanding evaluation practice. As a result, the *Albuquerque Journal* is writing a story about your evaluation system.

You agree to be interviewed by one of the newspaper's reporters. In your interview you describe what this evaluation system does, how it works, the kinds of information it collects, who uses the information, and how the information is used. Discuss what you would tell the reporter.

The following is a sample of what participants identified as a vision for what evaluation would look like in five years:

- Stakeholders are engaged and 100% onboard
- Processes and procedures are well documented, understood, and readily available

*(Continued)*

(Continued)

- We've won the Baldridge award
- Qualitative data are easily captured/compiled, interpreted
- We report meaningful data that prove our effectiveness and worth to SNL
- We are a universal corporate benchmark
- Evaluation is embedded in everyday work
- Evaluations are specific to the intervention
- Evaluation processes are well managed, funded, and part of corporate business process
- Data was collected by 100% of participants because of our easy to use system
- Data are reviewed regularly by stakeholders and acted upon—plan of action
- Data are interpreted accurately

The groups spent approximately 20 minutes sharing their themes and discussing the ideas generated from this phase. As participants left for lunch, the conversation was lively and upbeat. The department manager commented that she thought this process was a great way to get everyone involved and engaged. Some participants were also overhead saying, "This process is energizing," "It's refreshing to be looking at all the things we do well," and, "Thank you for including me in this meeting; I feel like I'm contributing."

When participants returned from lunch, they began the *Innovate* phase where they were asked to develop concrete statements that describe a current desirable state. During this phase, participants, in their groups of six, developed provocative propositions that addressed the organization's structure, culture, policies, leadership, management practices, systems, strategies, staff, and resources when it was involved in effective evaluation practice. The following are some of the provocative propositions they developed:

- Evaluation findings are commonly used for decision-making purposes
- All evaluation data are managed by our technical system that provides easily accessible reports to the desktop
- We use evaluation tools that collect reliable and valid data
- There is a database structure of meaningful core questions and the flexibility for customized questions for each product deliverable
- Data are automatically analyzed and "fixes" are suggested
- Reports may be generated using parameters such as course, session, date, and anything else that returns appropriate reports to the person requesting the information
- CEDT employs a full-time in-house evaluation team (n=5; including team lead) as a corporate resource for all types of interventions/assessments/evaluations
- "Evaluation" is socialized as a common language across Sandia
- Results are reported monthly through multiple channels
- The system accommodates both quantitative and qualitative data

- We send evaluation data to the managers who sent employees to a course to show the effectiveness, what we have learned, how we're changing in response
- CEDT management creates a business case with return on investment to secure funding and full-time equivalents

Since the evaluators were contracted to develop the evaluation system, the fourth and final phase, *Implement,* was modified. Participants were asked to do the following in their original pairs:

Review the provocative propositions and develop three to five recommendations for what would need to happen to make any of these provocative propositions come true. Join the other two pairs you have been working with and share your recommendations. Summarize your group's recommendations on a piece of flip-chart paper.

This activity was important because it prepared participants to consider what would need to be done after the final report was delivered.

At the end of the day, participants were asked to reflect on their experience. They offered the following comments:

- The day was worthwhile.
- I loved this process, this was great, we should use this more often.
- It's such a good idea to get a broad spectrum of ideas and this process did that with minimal effort.
- It seems like the only limitation to this process may be the participant's own ability to imagine.
- It's amazing how creative we can be when we're asked.
- I'd like to use this process more often and with other projects.
- I was inspired by the process and the fact that the managers supported this day.

As was requested by the client, a final report and executive summary were written. The report included a matrix describing all of the current forms and methods that were being used to collect evaluation data, a list of survey software vendors that the CEDT Department might want to consider, a model of an effective evaluation system, and eleven recommendations for implementing the evaluation system.

Shortly after the evaluators delivered the executive summary and final report, the CEDT Department formed a four-person evaluation team that was made up of representatives from each of the three divisions and the manager of Technical and Compliance Training. Their first task was to carefully review and discuss each of the recommendations contained within the report. After considering these recommendations and the CEDT comprehensive evaluation system, the CEDT evaluation team identified four areas on which to focus their next steps:

1. Education

2. Process/systems/technology

*(Continued)*

(Continued)

3. Strategic planning

4. Evaluation success/completion criteria

Each member invited others to be part of a sub-team to design and implement initiatives related to their particular focus area. As a result of the team's efforts, the CEDT Department has

- Implemented a requirement that evaluation sub-teams report on their progress at quarterly Department meetings
- Conducted an analysis of the capabilities of various software packages in an effort to find one that has advanced capabilities such as online delivery, database methodology, skip logic, and optical character recognition
- Purchased an online survey software system that met selected criteria
- Trained 10 individuals within the CEDT to use the new survey tool and assist with the pilot
- Conducted two focus group interviews, inviting all CEDT members to assess the need for data collected through end of course surveys
- Developed a revised end of course survey form to be used with all classroom-based courses
- Hosted a full-day online evaluation forum for the entire department on how to measure the value of online learning
- Developed an online evaluation course that is aligned with American Evaluation Association and International Society for Performance Improvement evaluation standards

In the end, the evaluators believe that using Appreciative Inquiry turned out to be not only an extremely cost-effective means for identifying and designing the system's essential elements, but engaging most of the department's members in the AI processes both reflected, and contributed to, the organization's desire to be a learning organization. Feedback from the department's leadership indicates that the evaluation system is being used and other Appreciative Inquiries are being implemented.

---

## Case Study 14

### Building an Evaluation System for the Conflict Resolution System of the World Bank Group[3]

The World Bank Group (WBG) has in place a Conflict Resolution System (CRS) that is comprised of five offices: Office of the Ombudsman, Office of Ethics and Business Conduct, Office of Mediation, the Appeals Committee, and the Administrative Tribunal. The first two offices (Ombudsman and Mediation) are responsible for informal resolution processes, the Office of Ethics addresses both informal and formal processes, and the Appeals and Tribunal offices deal with more formal conflict resolution processes. This approach to conflict resolution emphasizes informal, non-adversarial, problem-solving mechanisms with multiple channels and entry points focused on prevention and conflict resolution by first parties. The primary mission of the CRS is to promote constructive means of conflict resolution, ensure employees understand their ethical obligations, and expand the skills of the employees to address these issues at the WBG.

CRS employees' experience with evaluation was mostly limited to participation in a lengthy Annual Staff Survey, which covered a wide range of staff issues. This survey included questions regarding the use of and satisfaction with CRS services. One of the CRS offices had also been regularly implementing an exit survey of its users. The CRS offices were now interested in creating an evaluation system that could be implemented consistently across the five offices, while enabling each office to tailor evaluation activities to its specific needs and requirements. A lot of work had already gone into developing a case tracking system, which included a typology of cases, so they could track the different types of cases that came to the CRS. Consequently, the CRS managers had already been thinking about defining their work in ways they could use for evaluation purposes, so they could report to the WBG staff and Board about their work.

To begin developing the evaluation system, the evaluator planned and facilitated a 4-hour meeting with the five managers of the five CRS offices and a representative from the Human Resources Vice President's Office in order to explore the potential scope of the evaluation system (e.g., what types of evaluation activities might be included, what aspects of the CRS might be evaluated, what data collection methods might work most effectively with the CRS population and its constituents, and how evaluation activities might be sequenced). The meeting's agenda was as follows:

- AI into exceptional experiences of the CRS (*Inquire*)
- Stakeholder analysis
- Vision for the CRS (*Imagine*)
- Desired outcomes of the CRS
- Desired knowledge from the evaluation
- Elements of the evaluation system

During the AI in exceptional experiences, the evaluator asked the managers to interview each other in pairs on the following question (*Inquire*):

Reflect on your work experience at the CRS and remember a high point or peak experience you have had in your office—a time when you felt most alive, most engaged and excited about what you were doing. Tell me a story about that experience. What happened? What was your role? What role did others play? What made this possible? What were the key factors of success?

What do you most value about yourself? About the work you do? About the CRS?

*(Continued)*

(Continued)

> If you had three wishes for the CRS that would make more of these excep-
> tional experiences possible more of the time, what would they be?

The managers interviewed each other for a total of 30 minutes (15 minutes each)
and shared their stories of excellence, core values, and wishes for what would create more exceptional service provided by the CRS. The group then articulated the
themes that were emerging from the discussion. Notable among the themes was the
importance of having WBG staff understand the role and services of the CRS, and
WBG staff's trust in the confidentiality and independence of the CRS.

This was followed by a conversation to identify CRS stakeholders. The group discussed special issues that concerned each stakeholder group, their expectations of
the CRS, and the ways in which the CRS could assist them, and the organization, to
develop great "conflict competence." Next, the managers developed a vision of the
CRS in response to these questions (*Imagine* phase):

> Imagine that it is two years from now and you have just been recognized for
> the CRS' outstanding service at the WBG. What is going on that makes your
> services worthy of an award? What are staff saying about the CRS? What is hap-
> pening within the CRS? What are you doing that makes this possible?

Participants reflected individually and then shared their ideas in plenary. Reporting on
this question created a multi-dimensional vision that covered many CRS functions
and services, and represented a variety of perceptions and accomplishments. The
managers were then asked (*Innovate* phase):

> What are the key building blocks to work on in order to make the elements of
> this vision possible?

In response to this question, the group articulated the core functions and goals of the
CRS in a way that clearly set out the linkages between these functions and goals with
the overall mission of the CRS and stakeholders' needs. Their responses served as a
prelude to the final part of the meeting, which focused specifically on evaluation.

The final set of questions that the managers discussed in plenary were:

- In order to move toward this vision, to create these building blocks, and to
  enable the CRS to create more exceptional experiences for the WBG, what
  questions does evaluation need to answer for you?
- What information should evaluation provide?
- What learning should evaluation support?

By this time, the participants were ready to discuss their ideas for an evaluation system. Although none of the managers had an evaluation background, the Appreciative
Inquiry process and the spirited discussion that preceded these questions helped
them create links between the evaluation system they were creating and CRS'

mission, goals, and services. As a result, the managers were beginning to view evaluation as a vehicle for learning about their own performance, and for reporting to their stakeholders. They also agreed on the values that needed to be honored by evaluation practice within the CRS: respect for confidentiality, transparency, accountability, constructive feedback, collaboration among CRS managers, and staying within the scope of CRS services. In particular, the managers wanted the evaluation system to

- Provide ongoing information about CRS services, including
  - Information on the use of CRS services by different client groups.
  - Timely feedback from users of CRS services on their satisfaction with the process.
  - Changes in staff awareness of CRS services.
  - Staff perceptions of CRS's effectiveness.
- Support the needs of CRS managers in their decision-making practices:
  - Determine the effectiveness of CRS's training, education, outreach, and awareness services.
  - Determine the extent to which WBG staff are developing conflict competence.
  - Determine the effect of pilot programs on staff and management.
  - Determine the evolving needs of WBG staff in their developing conflict competence and link it to the CRS strategic plan.
- Provide various means for reporting:
  - Weekly reports to the Board
  - Annual CRS Report
  - Periodic reports on special issues
- Provide regular reviews on the adequacy and appropriateness of the evaluation system.

Following this meeting, the evaluator drafted a strategic plan for the evaluation system that included

- A flowchart of CRS functions, processes, outcomes, and goals
- A matrix outlining the evaluation information that the CRS wanted its evaluation system to answer, how the system would provide the information, from which information sources, through what evaluation methods, and at what time intervals
- A methods matrix that presented the methods that would be used by each part of the information system

The evaluator then met with the group several times to review the strategic plan. The managers clarified the potential use and utility of each type of evaluation activity listed in the evaluation strategic plan, considered the cost of each evaluation activity, and then prioritized evaluation activities according to their importance, practicality, and cost.

*(Continued)*

┌─ (Continued) ─────────────────────────────────────────────────┐

Incorporating Appreciative Inquiry into developing the CRS' evaluation system added significant value to the process. AI helped to honor and respect the unique values of the CRS. It helped the managers think of evaluation as a constructive rather than punitive process. And, most of all, it created a link between the program's goals and desired outcomes, and evaluation, in a way that felt exciting, comfortable, and interesting for CRS managers. After the system was agreed to, two CRS managers and the evaluator presented their work at the Association for Conflict Resolution Annual Conference. Those present at the conference session commented that Appreciative Inquiry is philosophically consistent with the values of conflict resolution. This realization made evaluation even more attractive to them.

└────────────────────────────────────────────────────────────────┘

## Summary

This chapter has emphasized that an organization will benefit most significantly from evaluative inquiry when there is a system to guide the design and implementation of all evaluation studies. Essential elements of an evaluation system include an evaluation strategic plan that articulates an evaluation vision and mission, the necessary financial and personnel resources, an evaluation plan for each inquiry, technological resources to support the collection of data and the dissemination of findings, and the leadership to support ongoing learning from evaluation. All of these elements contribute to obtaining useful and relevant information for organizational decision making. This chapter further described how Appreciative Inquiry can be used to help an organization design a functional and meaningful evaluation system. This is a particularly fitting application of AI because of its focus on whole-systems and strategic thinking. In addition, using Appreciative Inquiry to develop an evaluation system creates clear linkages between programmatic goals, desired outcomes, and the purpose and scope of the evaluation.

## Notes

1. An earlier version was developed with Barbra Zuckerman Portzline, PRISM Evaluation Consulting Services, Albuquerque, NM. Reprinted with permission.

2. The evaluation was conducted by PRISM Evaluation Consulting Services, Albuquerque, NM. An earlier version of this case was published in an issue of the *AI Practitioner,* February 2005. Reprinted with permission.

3. The evaluation was conducted by EnCompass LLC, Potomac, MD. Reprinted with permission.

# Building Evaluation Capacity Through Appreciative Inquiry $6$

> *Celebrate what you want more of.*
>
> —Anonymous

This final chapter highlights the ways in which Appreciative Inquiry can contribute to building organization and evaluation capacity. After providing some definitions and reasons for building capacity, it illustrates how using Appreciative Inquiry within an evaluation context builds evaluation capacity with two case examples. The chapter concludes by describing eight ways in which AI specifically contributes to building organization members' evaluation capacity.

## Building Organizational Capacity

It is nearly impossible to pick up a book on management or leadership without reading introductory statements about the changing nature of the workplace and the new strategies needed for organizational success. Whether they focus on changes caused by global competition, shrinking resources, more powerful and accessible technologies, an increasingly diverse workforce, the shift from an industrial to a knowledge economy, or new state and federal regulations and requirements, the message is clear—organizations need to be flexible, fast, adaptable, and innovative (Redding & Catalanello, 1994; Schwandt & Marquardt, 2000). In other words, they must evolve in ways that contribute to their own growth, financial health, productivity, and overall success over a sustained period of time.

In the nonprofit, health, education, and government arenas in particular, building organizational capacity has become a key strategy for addressing the continuing challenges of succeeding in a volatile and fluid work environment. Briefly, organizational capacity building refers to

- An organization's ability to achieve its mission effectively and to sustain itself over the long term. (Alliance for Nonprofit Management, n.d.)

- Any process that increases the capability of individuals to produce or perform . . . capacity building enables all stakeholders to carry out their tasks to the best of their ability. (North Central Regional Educational Laboratory, n.d.)

- An organisation's capacity is its potential to perform—its ability to successfully apply its skills and resources toward the accomplishment of its goals and the satisfaction of its stakeholders' expectations. The aim of capacity development is to improve the organisation's performance by increasing its potential in terms of its resources and management. (de Souza Silva, 2003, p. 3)

Building organizational capacity often involves efforts to manage change, resolve conflict, foster communication, align and coordinate various organizational functions and processes, create a learning culture, and share knowledge. In other words, building organizational capacity includes

Activities that improve an organization's ability to achieve its mission or a person's ability to define and realize his/her goals or to do his/her job more effectively. For organizations, capacity building may relate to almost any aspect of its work: improved governance, leadership, mission and strategy, administration (including human resources, financial management, and legal matters), program development and implementation, fundraising and income generation, diversity, partnerships and collaboration, evaluation, advocacy and policy change, marketing, positioning, planning, etc. For individuals, capacity building may relate to leadership development, advocacy skills, training/ speaking abilities, technical skills, organizing skills, and other areas of personal and professional development. (The Alliance for Nonprofit Management, n.d.)

Strategies for building organizational capacity include (1) augmenting the skills and competencies of an organization's individual members and leaders; (2) strengthening the organization's systems; and (3) fostering a culture that enables the organization to do its work well over time. By working at these three levels (individual, system, and culture), organizations can address the challenges they face more effectively and to move strategically toward success. For many nonprofit organizations, organizational capacity building is a way to leverage limited resources (Connolly & York, 2002), which, in times of rapid and unpredictable changes, is critically important for organizational survival. As the pace of change has increased, building organizational capacity has required approaches that help all organizations improve their ability to "read" important changes in their environments and to respond faster.

Over the years, many approaches have emerged that target building capacity. These include Total Quality Management, the Balanced Score Card, Future Search conferences, Reengineering, corporate universities, technology solutions, and, of course, Appreciative Inquiry. Whichever approach is used, the goal is to increase an organization's effectiveness—to build the capacity of the organization to succeed.

## Evaluation's Contribution to Organizational Capacity Building

Evaluation can enhance an organization's ability to collect, process, and analyze data about change within and outside the organization, and to draw important lessons that enable the organization to adapt appropriately and address that changing environment. Thus, evaluation contributes to the organization's ability to learn by enhancing its members' competencies and by enabling it to make smart adaptations to its systems as needed. Organizational learning, which became popular in the early 1990s as a result of Peter Senge's book, *The Fifth Discipline*, has been defined in different ways by many authors. Senge (1990) suggests that organizational learning occurs in "organizations where people continually expand their capacity to create the results they truly desire, where new and expansive patterns of thinking are nurtured, where collective aspiration is set free, and where people are continually learning how to learn together" (p. 3). Dixon (1994) adds to Senge's definition by linking three elements that are critical for learning—individual and organizational learning and learning systems: "Organizational learning is the intentional use of learning processes at the individual, group and system level to continuously transform the organization in a direction that is increasingly satisfying to its stakeholders" (p. 5). Common themes found in various definitions of organizational learning include

- Increased knowledge will improve action.
- Inquiry is fundamental to creating knowledge.
- There is a profound relationship between the organization and its environment.
- There is a desire for continuous improvement.
- It is a means for creating organizational change.

Furthermore, organizational learning most often occurs when there is a jolt or trigger that signals a major threat to the survival of the institution, there is little time to react to new external or internal requirements (e.g., new ideas, new vision, new competition, new regulations or requirements), and/or the crisis confronting the organization has not been anticipated. In part, such a crisis spurs organizational learning because it forces organization members to look at the situation anew—to change their frame of reference and search for innovative and creative ways to address pressing issues and challenges.

Evaluation has the potential to help organizations see themselves with new eyes through the process of evaluative inquiry. In today's ever-changing organizational environments, evaluation can play a critical role for helping an organization inquire into and learn about what it is doing well in addition to understanding where it needs to improve and change. In this respect, evaluation contributes to developing organizational capacity by providing information that can be used to enhance or maximize the organization's performance (Preskill and Torres, 1999).

Consequently, evaluation can contribute to organizational capacity building by

- Providing greater clarity about the organization's goals, objectives, strategies, activities, and expected outcomes that make explicit the internal logic of programs and activities, thus enabling greater agreement and alignment within an organization

- Enabling the organization to make decisions based on more accurate information and analysis that helps them make adjustments to their products and services

- Increasing the organization's accountability to its members, customers, and stakeholders so that they can report their progress and learning more accurately and effectively

- Creating more transparency as more is known about operations and performance; evaluation provides opportunities to foster a culture of openness, empowerment, and learning

- Increasing organization members' skills in engaging in evaluative inquiry and evaluative thinking in their daily work

Ultimately, organizations need to consider developing an evaluation system that institutionalizes evaluation and promotes evaluative thinking among its members. By participating actively in evaluation, organizations emphasize the link between asking questions (inquiry) and improving practice and, as a result, are better positioned to use evaluation findings and embed evaluation practices into their culture and work processes.

## Building Evaluation Capacity

As organizations have worked to build the capacity of their members to achieve higher levels of performance, so too have evaluators sought ways to build organization members' capacity to learn about and use evaluation processes and findings within the context of their work. Evaluation capacity building (ECB) is about enabling organizations to allocate resources for evaluation, increasing members' evaluation competencies, and sustaining evaluation and evaluative thinking as a way of life in the organization. ECB has been defined in a number of ways. For example, Stockdill, Baizerman, and Compton (2002) describe it as "a context-dependent, intentional action system of guided processes and practices for bringing about and sustaining a state of affairs in which quality program evaluation and its appropriate uses are ordinary and ongoing practices within and/or between one or more organizations/programs/sites" (p. 8).

Highlighting the importance of an organization's infrastructure, Gibbs, Napp, Jolly, Westover, and Uhl (2002) define evaluation capacity building as "The extent to which an organization has the necessary resources and motivation to conduct, analyze, and use evaluations" (p. 261). Specifically, building evaluation capacity helps organizations

- Record and report results
- Meet accountability demands
- Align various processes and continuous improvement initiatives
- Support efforts to acquire new or additional funding
- Enhance an organization's ability to become a learning organization
- Increase the ability to gather and use information for decision making
- Use external consultants efficiently and effectively
- Value the knowledge and skills of internal members

To help organizations build their evaluation capacity, evaluators strive to conceptualize, design, and sustain ongoing evaluation practices that are linked to the organization's strategic mission and goals. By connecting evaluation to other forms of organizational inquiry and decision making, they try to make evaluation relevant to organizational life. When evaluation is seen as useful—when evaluation findings are used—organizational members are more likely to devote resources to evaluation and to develop evaluation knowledge and skills in the organization. Ultimately, evaluators seek to integrate evaluation practice with the organization's systems, structures, and culture.

To build evaluation capacity, evaluators may use the occasion of conducting a specific evaluation to teach participants to (a) develop a program's logic model, (b) develop key evaluation questions, (c) identify the evaluation's stakeholders and their intended use of findings, (d) develop effective data collection methods and instruments, (e) analyze and interpret data, and (f) communicate and report an evaluation's findings. Sometimes, this may mean significantly changing organization members' perception of the nature of evaluation. It is not unusual to hear managers suggest that evaluation is limited to assessment and testing by outside experts—that is, the collection of quantitative data and the production of statistical results. The following quote, from a book on organizational learning and change, illustrates this situation:

> In conventional assessments, experts produce recommendations through a kind of "black box." . . . The evaluators collect the data (the amount you spent and the quantifiable benefits), plug it into formulas (perhaps return on investment, cash flow, or internal rate of return), and produce a quick quantifiable judgment, perhaps based on a hurdle rate or ROI calculation. (Roth, 1999, p. 303)

Further supporting the perception that evaluation is driven and defined by the scientific method, Watkins and Mohr (2001) write,

> Even though these days most traditional evaluations point out successes and failure uncovered in an evaluation process, it seem to be human nature to focus on, if not obsess about, those things that others declare (or that we ourselves fear) do not measure up to some standard assumed to define "perfection." . . . We would argue that applying scientific methods of the Newtonian paradigm to human systems is flawed at best, if not actually a useless endeavor. (p. 182)

These statements bespeak the significant biases that clients frequently bring to an evaluation. In order to conduct a more effective and participatory evaluation, evaluators frequently need to help clients see evaluation more broadly. To build organization members' evaluation capacity, evaluators need to help them see evaluation as a critically important learning process. The learning that occurs from participating in the evaluation has been called *process use* by Patton (1997). He defines process use as

> individual changes in thinking and behavior, and program or organizational changes in procedures and culture, that occur among those involved in evaluation as a result of the learning that occurs during the evaluation process. Evidence of process use is represented by the following kind of statement after an evaluation: "The impact on our program came not just from the findings but from going through the thinking process that the evaluation required." (p. 90)

Process use is grounded in social constructivist learning theory, which suggests that individuals construct knowledge and develop a shared reality through their interactions with others. It is through participants' construction, interpretation, and integration of past experiences that new knowledge is developed (Bruner, 1971; Campbell, 2000; Lave & Wenger, 1991). In their exploratory research study on process use, Preskill, Zuckerman, and Matthews (2003) identified five categories of variables that appear to affect process use: (1) Facilitation of Evaluation Processes, (2) Management Support, (3) Advisory Group Characteristics, (4) Frequency, Methods, and Quality of Communications, and (5) Organization Characteristics (p. 430). When evaluation studies pay attention to these variables and are intentional about participants' learning, greater process use (i.e., learning from the evaluation process) is likely to take place.

Appreciative Inquiry contributes to building evaluation capacity by enabling a more effective facilitation of evaluation, engaging management support, creating more effective communications about the evaluation, and helping to reframe negative perceptions about evaluation. To illustrate how AI contributes to building evaluation capacity, we provide two case examples. In the first example, AI was used to build the evaluation capacity of a U.S.-based nonprofit organization and its five nonprofit partners based in five European countries. This is an organization whose staff were not trained in evaluation, and who were coached in record time to deliver an outstanding evaluation workshop to their partners. The second case example focuses on how evaluation capacity was developed with project staff in one of Chile's health quality assurance programs.

---

**Case Study 15**

## Building Evaluation Capacity in the Women's Empowerment Program in Five Eastern European Countries[1]

IREX is a nonprofit organization primarily focused on capacity building of overseas nonprofit organizations by bringing nonprofit leaders from developing countries to the United States and other countries for training on a range of management and international development topics. IREX had been implementing a Labor Department three-year contract titled Eastern Europe Women's Empowerment Program. The goal of this training and coaching program was to increase young women's employability and self-confidence in order to prevent their involvement in human trafficking. The program was being implemented in Bulgaria, Moldova, Lithuania, Russia, and Serbia through five different local nonprofit organizations (one for each country).

The Department of Labor funded an independent mid-term evaluation that recommended the inclusion of additional impact indicators in the project's logic model and final report. The project only had six months remaining before completion, and IREX staff were very concerned that adding indicators at such a late stage in the project would set up the project for failure. They were wondering how they would be able to show any impact on the new indicators, and whether this

*(Continued)*

(Continued)

requirement would diminish the importance of the project's many accomplishments. They were also worried about the response they would receive from the five local Non-Governmental Organization (NGO) partners regarding collecting additional impact data, since there had always been some resistance to directives from the American headquarters. Furthermore, the IREX staff did not have a background in evaluation design or data collection and analysis, so they were unsure of what to do. They had already planned to have their partner NGOs conduct one last telephone survey and thought the survey might be a good way to collect information on the newly required indicators that would be developed. They also knew they would need to train their foreign partners on how to administer the survey, and how to manage the logistics of translating the survey into their local languages, recording responses, translating the survey data back into English, and transmitting the results to IREX headquarters.

To help them with these tasks, IREX contracted with an evaluation consulting firm to (a) develop new impact indicators, (b) develop a training program for teaching their partners how to conduct surveys, (c) develop data collection methods and related instruments, and (d) coach IREX staff to facilitate the evaluation workshop.

**Reasons for Using AI**

Because of the staff's history with evaluation and the short timeline, the evaluation consultants decided to use Appreciative Inquiry for three reasons:

1. The IREX staff did not have a positive view of evaluation. In large part, this was due to the Department of Labor's midterm evaluation that, in their view, had failed to capture the project's accomplishments sufficiently. The evaluation team was confident that AI would capture those accomplishments and make evaluation a positive and energizing experience.

2. The IREX staff were experiencing evaluation as a negative burden on their workload, as they felt under pressure to add new impact indicators, revise and administer their survey so they could gather new impact data, and train and motivate their partner NGOs to respond to the survey. The evaluation team believed that AI would enable IREX staff to translate fairly easily their vision of desired outcomes into a logical framework, and to develop exciting indicators linked to those outcomes. Also, the evaluation team wanted to help the IREX staff understand that evaluation could be a positive learning experience that added value to their work.

3. The IREX staff wanted to develop the staff's capacity to conduct evaluations, as they would be training their partner NGOs and also analyzing the data themselves. The evaluation team believed that AI would help IREX staff internalize evaluative thinking, and give them the tools to train and motivate their NGO partners to participate in the evaluation effort.

## Focusing the Evaluation

The evaluation team decided to begin the process by involving the four IREX staff in an AI *focusing meeting* to identify and clarify the project's desired outcomes and achievements. The goal of this session was to revise the logic model included in IREX's original proposal into a new one that included impact indicators, which would then enable IREX to collect impact data from their overseas partner NGOs and report them back to the funding agency. The evaluation team felt confident that using AI would help IREX staff articulate, capture, and document these accomplishments, gain a perspective for the rest of the evaluation, get excited about collecting data in the future, recognize that there are things that can be evaluated successfully, and make them more open to evaluation. In a 3-hour session, the staff members responded to the following appreciative questions in plenary (no paired interviews were held because of the small group size):

- Reflect for a moment and remember an exceptional or "best" experience you have had with the Women's Programs. Tell me a story about that experience. What made it the best? Who else was involved? What role did you play? What role did others play?
- What were the key factors that helped make it an exceptional experience?
- Values: What do you most value about
  - Yourself—without being humble, what is it about yourself that you most value (as a person or citizen or partner/spouse or parent—in any role you wish to speak to)?
  - The work that you do?
  - The organization you are part of?
- If you had three wishes that would ensure that the work in the Women's Programs is as exceptional as the one you have described, what would they be?

## Building Staff Capacity

After the meeting, the evaluation team worked closely with the IREX staff to revise their logic model (which was renamed to *results framework*) based on the staff's exciting, yet realistic, desired outcomes. The new logic model focused on results, and began with goals, desired outcomes, intermediate results, strategies, and project activities. It also redefined the project's components to capture some of accomplishments that the project's staff were most proud of. The new results framework identified intermediate and long-term outcomes that the project was trying to achieve.

Using the new results framework, the evaluation team helped the IREX staff redesign a previously used survey instrument so that it would capture the intermediate impact results that were possible at that stage of the project. Specifically, the survey was revised to (a) reflect a better alignment with the new results framework and indicators and (b) include some appreciative questions. The survey was to be administered by IREX's partner NGOs in the field.

With the revised results framework and survey instrument, IREX staff now had to direct and train their partner NGOs on how to administer the survey. Two IREX staff members were due to conduct this evaluation capacity workshop with their partner

*(Continued)*

(Continued)

NGOs at a Moscow conference later that month. They asked the evaluation team to help them design an agenda for the evaluation portion of the workshop. The evaluation team developed a series of activities that incorporated AI into addressing the evaluation's goals, revised framework, survey, data collection procedures, and next steps. The following agenda was used for the daylong evaluation capacity workshop facilitated by IREX staff to their five partners in Moscow:

- *Honoring the Best of "What Is": The Unique Contribution of the Women's Project* using an appreciative guide as follows:
  - Reflect for a moment and remember a high point or an exceptional experience you have had in working with the Women's Empowerment Project—a time when you felt you were really making a contribution to the lives of the women and girls that you serve, a time when you felt you were really making a difference. Tell me a story about that experience.
  - What made it exceptional? What role did you play? What role did others play? What were the key factors that helped make it a peak experience?
  - What are the things you value deeply; specifically, the things you value about your work? When you are feeling best about your work, what do you value about it?
  - What do you think is the unique contribution of the Women's Empowerment Project to the field of human trafficking? What sets it apart?
  - If you had three wishes that would ensure that more of these exceptional experiences would be possible more of the time, what would they be?

- *Whose Voice is Missing?* Participants identified important program stakeholders.

- *Perspectives on Monitoring and Evaluation.* Participants discussed their views of monitoring and evaluation, and the challenge of collecting data.

- *Documenting Our Success.* Participants made links between evaluation and its role in honoring the work and successes of the program and its participants, the difference it is making in girls' lives, the resources devoted to the program, and ways for improving and expanding the program. By the end of this session, participants created a list of impact indicators.

- *The Follow-Up Survey.* Participants reviewed the survey they were asked to implement, planned the implementation of the survey, discussed strategies for handling difficult questions and situations, practiced using the survey, and provided feedback on improving it.

- *Focus Groups.* Participants practiced conducting focus group interviews.

- *Monitoring and Evaluation Next Steps.* Participants developed the plan for collecting, recording, and transmitting the data to IREX headquarters.

- *Closing: Envisioning the Future.* Participants reflected on what they learned together, affirmed their commitment to evaluation, and concluded the workshop.

Prior to the Moscow trip, the evaluation team coached the IREX staff in a half-day training session on how to facilitate the workshop. With their new results framework, survey, evaluation curriculum, and coaching, they left for Moscow.

### Results

When they returned from the Moscow workshop, the IREX staff reported success beyond their expectations. They said that one local trainer who attended the workshop said that this was the best training she had ever attended. IREX was also pleased to have a revised logic model for its *Eastern Europe Women's Empowerment Program* incorporating impact indicators in record time, in a way that satisfied the Department of Labor. The IREX staff became increasingly energized about evaluation and were satisfied that the local NGOs were on board and excited to administer the survey and record the impact of the project. According to IREX's May 2003 newsletter, a participant summarized that the local NGO partners had gained a "new attitude towards cooperation with NGOs and government agencies." This is noteworthy in a workshop that was conducted in six different languages (including English) by staff who were not trained as trainers or evaluators. Using Appreciative Inquiry made this possible.

### Benefits of Using AI

Ultimately, using AI helped the IREX staff build not only their own evaluation capacity but also contributed to increasing the evaluation capacity of their local nonprofit partners in five countries. Through their use of Appreciative Inquiry, the IREX staff connected the goals of the program to the important mission of preventing the trafficking of girls, and developed a results framework, a set of meaningful indicators, and companion data collection instruments. By using AI, they were able to reframe their previously negative experiences with evaluation into viewing evaluation as an opportunity to forge renewed connections with overseas partners (in the Moscow training), and become an activity that contributes to learning and confidence building. As a result of this activity, the IREX staff transformed their understanding of evaluation and increased their capacity to engage in future evaluations.

---

**Case Study 16**

## Building Evaluation Capacity in Chile's Health Quality Assurance Program[2]

In this case example, Appreciative Inquiry was used both as an evaluation methodology and as a means for building the evaluation capacity of Chile's health quality assurance program. From 1996–2001, University Research Co., LLC (URC) implemented an international Quality Assurance Project (QAP) funded by the United States Agency for International Development. The project's purpose was to test and refine quality assurance methods and tools designed to improve the quality of healthcare delivery in 15 developing countries. One of the project's required deliverables was an evaluation methodology that could be used by health managers and evaluators to evaluate health quality assurance services. A particular requirement of the project was to field test innovative methods for conducting such evaluations.

*(Continued)*

(Continued)

As a result, evaluations of the quality assurance activities were undertaken in Zambia, Niger, and Chile.

**Using Appreciative Inquiry**

In Chile, the evaluators decided to test the use of Appreciative Inquiry for collecting data. Two of the 12 sites the evaluators visited used an Appreciative Inquiry process to evaluate the country's quality improvement activities (see Catsambas, Kelley, Legros, Massoud, & Brouchet, 2002, for a more detailed description of the different evaluation methods tested). Because one of the purposes of the emerging evaluation methodology was to make it useful for quality assurance managers and local evaluators, the evaluation team wanted to include methods that would be culturally responsive, appropriate, and empowering to these users.

In preparation for the site visits, the evaluator designed an appreciative interview guide that scripted how a Chilean evaluator/facilitator was to introduce each part of the process. A Chilean physician who was working with the program was asked to conduct the 2½ hour appreciative interview session with groups of nurses who were responsible for implementing the quality improvement activities. The evaluation team decided to ask a local resident to conduct the interviews since the evaluators visiting Chile had no background in Appreciative Inquiry, and they wanted to see how the approach worked with minimal outside intervention. The following agenda, which guided the interview session, reflects the *Inquire* phase of the AI process:

- Introduction (5 minutes)
- Paired interviews (90 minutes each)
- Sharing of stories at tables (30 minutes)
- Sharing of stories with the whole group (10 minutes)
- Developing themes from their stories at tables (15 minutes)
- Reporting out and exploration of themes—key findings (15 minutes)
- Group discussion: Reflecting on the meaning of the findings (5 minutes)
- Listing and prioritizing wishes—recommendations (10 minutes)

Participants interviewed each other in pairs. Because it was recognized that participants might not have had the same type of peak experience and it was important to explore several key aspects of the project, they were given a choice of answering one or two of the following questions plus question set D, which everyone was asked to answer.

*Continuous Process Improvement (A)*

- Think back on your experience with quality assurance process improvement activities in your time here. Remember a time and tell a story about a high point or peak experience you had with any aspect of continuous process improvement. What happened? What role did you play? How were others involved? Why was significant about this experience? Who were the clients of this high-point experience? How were they affected? What was the best thing for the clients or patients?

*Problem Solving (B)*

- An important activity in Quality Improvement is Problem Solving. Remember a time and tell a story about a high point or peak experience that you had in problem solving. What happened? What role did you play? How were others involved? What quality assurance tools were most helpful to you? What was the outcome? Who were the clients of this high point? How were they affected? What was the best thing for the clients or patients?

*Teamwork (C)*

- Teamwork is frequently very important in quality assurance. Remember a time and tell a story about a high point or peak experience in working with a team. What happened? What was your role? What did you contribute to the team? What role did others play? What was the outcome? What was the best thing that happened or that worked in that team? What training (medical, quality assurance, or other) best helped you or others to operate in this successful team?

*Values and Wishes (D)*

- What do you most value about yourself?
- What do you most value about your work in healthcare?
- What do you most value about your work in quality assurance?
- If you had one wish that would make it possible for you to have more of these high points or peak experiences in your work, what would that wish be?

At the end of the interview session, participants were asked to complete a survey that asked for their feedback on the use of Appreciative Inquiry to conduct these evaluation related interviews. They were asked to compare it to their experience with the interview guide that was used for data collection in other sites (and had been developed through previous evaluations). The Chilean physician who facilitated the appreciative interviews was also asked to complete an evaluation form. Her feedback was deemed particularly important since she had been involved in previous evaluations using non-AI methods. Finally, the U.S.-based team that traveled to Chile to manage the evaluation was also given a survey that asked for its feedback comparing previously used non-AI interview questions and the use of the appreciative interview questions.

**Feedback on Using AI**

Based on all of the feedback obtained, there was consensus that both the non-AI interview guide that was used in other sites and the Appreciative Inquiry process used in these two sites led to similar findings. This result was somewhat surprising to a few

*(Continued)*

(Continued)

of those involved in the evaluation, since there had been some initial skepticism about whether the appreciative questions would be able to capture significant findings. Importantly, everyone agreed that using Appreciative Inquiry had been exciting and engaging for all of the participants, which was encouraging since one of the evaluation's goals had been to identify innovative evaluation methods.

The Chilean participants who experienced the Appreciative Inquiry process decided to continue using it for future inquiries into organizational issues and challenges. They reported that it made sense to them intuitively, and they felt energized when applying it. They also saw the links it created between the evaluation questions and the information that it was generating; they were particularly surprised at how the appreciative questions produced such specific and useful information. In the end, the U.S.-based evaluation team concluded that the AI approach should be included in the *Evaluation Health Manager's Guide* that presented the overall methodology, because it would be useful for local evaluators and program managers.

Unexpectedly, this experience had an impact on the U.S.-based headquarters team of quality assurance experts in that it contributed to building their own evaluation capacity. After this application, project staff who managed activities throughout the world began using AI as a way to gather data in their operations research studies and in future evaluations. For example, the QAP project conducted an evaluation in Malawi where the evaluation manager decided to use Appreciative Inquiry because it made sense to her, and she thought the client would be responsive and likely to share more "real" information. She explained, "You learn the important things about a program in the hallway, on your way to your next formal meeting; AI brings this hallway storytelling into the official meeting."

## Appreciative Inquiry's Contributions to Building Organizational and Evaluation Capacity

The previous chapters have covered ways in which evaluation can be enhanced by incorporating AI. The experiences of those who use Appreciative Inquiry in evaluations have shown that it contributes to building organizational and evaluation capacity in seven ways (see Figure 6.1):

**1. Appreciative Inquiry reframes the study of problems to the study of successes.**

The AI process shifts evaluation from being a negative, blaming, fault-finding, problem-solving approach toward a form of inquiry that focuses on success, peak experiences, positive engagement, and creative opportunities. AI increases organization members' ability to reframe organizational issues and challenges, thus enhancing members' confidence and ability to tackle them.

After being part of an Appreciative Inquiry process, participants frequently report that, when facing a challenge, they find themselves asking, "What has it been like when we have been effective or successful in doing this in the past?" In other words, the nature of their questions and conversations

1. Reframes the study of problems to the study of successes

2. Emphasizes how evaluation can be a learning rather than a punitive process

3. Provides an option for more cost-effective evaluation

4. Contributes to culturally responsive evaluation by embracing diversity

5. Offers new language that allows greater honesty about difficult topics

6. Unleashes creativity through affirming, participatory, and energizing processes

7. Increases understanding of evaluation processes and findings, thus leading to greater use and influence

8. Complements systems thinking and complexity theory approaches

**Figure 6.1**    Contributions of Appreciative Inquiry to Building Organizational and Evaluation Capacity

about organizational challenges becomes reframed. They begin to approach challenges from a study of successful practice, and use that study to draw lessons for charting new directions. This is especially important in today's volatile and unpredictable work environment, where employees often become discouraged and overwhelmed by the many demands and constraints placed upon them. Even though many problem-solving approaches attempt to remove "blame" from the problem-solving process, it is often difficult for participants to avoid this behavior. The Appreciative Inquiry process more effectively eliminates one's tendency to assign blame since it reframes issues into possibilities based on past successes. Even when no one is blamed, the study of problems—including negative outcomes, system deficiencies, lack of resources, management and staff resistance, and other such causes of problems—makes it difficult to feel hopeful. By studying successes to resolve issues, participants arrive at solutions through a very different path, one that frees them to be innovative and hopeful about their visions of the future. This reframing aspect of AI helps reduce stress, increase confidence, and unleash creativity. In this way, AI builds organizational capacity to address issues at hand, and when AI is applied to evaluation, it also builds evaluation capacity because participants experience evaluation as a constructive and energizing learning process.

**2. Appreciative Inquiry emphasizes how evaluation can be a learning process rather than a punitive process.**

As such, AI demystifies evaluation, makes it less threatening, and increases organization members' motivation to participate in the evaluation.

Experienced evaluators often say that one of their greatest challenges is helping organization members overcome the perception that evaluation is threatening, unproductive, and adversarial. For example, one of the authors of this book who teaches an introductory graduate level evaluation course for students in the fields of training, K–12 education, organization development, and instructional technology begins the semester by asking students to draw a picture of "evaluation"—to sketch the image that comes to mind when they see or hear the word. She tells them they have just two minutes in which to draw their image and label it with one or two words. While some of the pictures represent neutral and positive images, such as a scale, a question mark, a checklist, and binoculars, there are far more negative images such as an axe, a test, someone being fired, a gun, and a hangman's noose (Preskill & Russ-Eft, 2005). What emerges is participants' sense of fear and/or resistance to evaluation. The fact is, most people have experienced a time when data were collected in the work environment under the guise of program improvement, only to find that the results were used to punish or fire employees, or to support a political agenda. To this point, Meador (1999) tells a story of when he was working at General Motors and the CEO insisted on collecting evaluative data on a regular basis. Meador writes, "When they didn't like the information, they called people on the carpet," at which time the CEO was known to yell, "I finally have the data to show that the people in manufacturing aren't doing their job!" (pp. 299–300). Not surprisingly, there was little trust in who was collecting data or how the data would be used.

In working with Appreciative Inquiry's core questions, when individuals are encouraged to think about and discuss their peak experiences relative to what is being evaluated, much of their fear or concern dissipates. For programs fraught with problems, participants begin timidly to look for success to study, as these successes might be exceptions; as they engage further in the inquiry, they begin to study these successes in earnest. The change in participants' energy level and engagement becomes palpable in this process. Participants approach evaluation expecting to be asked about their mistakes or failures, and their proposals for how to address these deficiencies. They are surprised to find themselves engaged in a process of thinking how best to proceed based on what has worked well and has been successful. This realization results in significant stress reduction, and creates a positive climate that typically leads to greater participation and investment in the evaluation process. Instead of avoiding uncomfortable and threatening discussions, participants find that they are energized with renewed hope and a sense of possibility for improved organizational performance. When the time comes to discuss what is needed that is not present, they are ready to fill perceived gaps not with deficiencies but with gifts and wishes. Consequently, evaluation becomes more accessible and less intimidating; they perceive it as a learning, rather than a punitive, process.

### 3. Appreciative Inquiry provides an option for more cost-effective evaluation.

It is no secret that evaluation studies can be labor intensive and time-consuming. As such, clients are often surprised when the evaluator explains how much an evaluation will cost in terms of personnel time and financial resources. Even for those clients who are fully supportive of the evaluation, many have not included evaluation expenses in their budget and, as a result, must find ways to cover the evaluation's cost.

In addition to the monetary cost, there are corresponding human resource costs—for example, the evaluation participants' time, which is essential to an evaluation's success. Evaluators find that program managers may be reluctant to make themselves or their staff accessible during the evaluation process. Competing priorities often delay or impede an evaluation's implementation, which may compromise the evaluation's success. And, for better or worse, organizations also want evaluations done quickly; many clients are not willing or able to spend three, six, nine months or longer conducting an evaluation. In many cases, however, Appreciative Inquiry can be used to collect a significant amount of data in a shorter time period. Using AI, the evaluator is able to bring together a large numbers of diverse stakeholders, rather than needing to conduct individual or focus group interviews. Consequently, AI can be a very efficient and effective method of data collection.

**4. Appreciative Inquiry contributes to culturally responsive evaluation by embracing diversity.**

Appreciative Inquiry is a participatory process that does not force consensus. It engages diverse stakeholders in structured storytelling through interviews, and preserves the language of each individual story throughout its process. As groups seek common ground in their insights about success, values, and future directions, their separate and distinct voices stay intact. These original, individual stories co-exist with the analysis and synthesis that follows and remain an essential piece of "the findings," helping to explain and interpret those findings through many different lenses at the same time. In this way, AI helps the organization get "smarter" by highlighting and validating different mental models held by its members and, in so doing, allows for the coexistence of many (and sometimes opposite) "truths."

AI also contributes to the evaluation's cultural responsiveness and its potential outcomes by ensuring that everyone's voice has equal time. Appreciative Inquiry begins this during the *Inquire* phase when participants are asked to interview another person using the core AI questions, which have been specifically tailored for the evaluation. Even those who are shy or reticent to speak in front of people they do not know are often more willing and comfortable talking with just one person. The interviews provide a relaxed setting for people to talk, and participants find it motivating to know that someone is listening carefully and with interest to their story. The paired interviews also serve as a means for each person to learn more about the program being evaluated, and each other's role with the program. As the *Inquire* phase continues, stories are retold and heard in groups of six or eight and, when time permits, in plenary. Stories are retold not by the original storyteller, but by others, making these stories part of the collective wisdom and knowledge base. The use of storytelling helps to surface opposing views in a safe environment, builds understanding, creates a context for individual views, and increases trust among participants. Increased trust with stakeholders also means greater honesty about issues and concerns, higher quality data, and increased buy-in to the evaluation process. Even when they do not agree, participants develop a heightened level of respect for others' views, values, and culture. At the end of the day, everyone has new understanding of how each individual adds value to the organization.

AI is particularly helpful for evaluations whose stakeholders come from diverse cultures. This diversity can be ethnic, religious, educational, geographic, gender, ability, position within the organization, and so on. AI helps bridge these differences through deepened understanding and insight. For evaluations in diverse cultural settings, AI allows the evaluator to stay in listening mode and to test assumptions about the cultural setting. Appreciative Inquiry has been used in many countries in Africa, Asia, Latin America, and Europe, and has been found to work well in these contexts. As countries increasingly collaborate in initiatives such as reducing poverty, decreasing the speed of global warming, protecting human rights, and fighting the spread of HIV/AIDS, it is critically important for evaluators to incorporate methods and tools that enable them to work effectively across cultures and in international settings. AI makes an important contribution for implementing culturally competent and internationally appropriate evaluations.

### 5. Appreciative Inquiry offers new language that allows greater honesty about difficult topics.

As participants identify examples of excellence and analyze exceptional experiences, they become ready to articulate their "wishes" of things that need to happen to enable their organization or program to operate at higher levels of excellence. This is particularly important when there are sensitive issues participants have not felt comfortable discussing in other forums. And unfortunately, "paying attention to what people talk about and what they don't talk about is often an overlooked key to organizational success" (Hammond & Mayfield, 2004, p. 26). The use of AI provides a safer and more open environment for addressing difficult issues by talking about successes. In this way, Appreciative Inquiry enables stakeholders to "discuss the undiscussables."

### 6. Appreciative Inquiry unleashes creativity through affirming, participatory, and energizing processes.

By engaging participants in an interactive, affirming, and whole-systems process, evaluation participants interact with each other in fresh and energizing ways. As they talk about things they value most in themselves and their work, they begin to appreciate their own and others' contributions to the organization's success and become animated when asked to suggest changes that build more success in their organization. This appreciative process of launching evaluation or collecting data makes intuitive sense to them, even though it is rather new for most. Participants tend to relax, become more reflective, playful, and open. When they participate in the *Innovate* phase, they are invited to be creative; they are asked to develop provocative propositions with bold ideas that stretch the imagination about building the desired future of their organization. By this time, evaluation participants frequently find themselves thinking "out of the box" and staying open-minded to the thoughts of others. The evaluation process thus becomes a forum for exchange of ideas and learning that participants end up owning. In this way, the highly interactive and engaging process of AI fosters risk taking, creativity, and innovation.

7. **Appreciative Inquiry increases understanding of evaluation processes and findings, thus leading to greater use and influence.**

Because of the great degree of participation and inclusion fostered by AI, participants are involved in defining and implementing the evaluation from the beginning. The appreciative aspect of the inquiry increases their buy-in to the process and their enthusiasm for implementing desired changes. Participants are intimately engaged in the evaluation work and thus are more likely to find the results credible. In addition, the evaluation's findings and recommendations have been derived from their own positive and successful experiences, which has strengthened participants' faith that they can succeed once again in their new ventures as they make changes outlined in the resulting action plan. Through AI, considerations of evaluation use are built in from the beginning. By being intentional about the use of results from the beginning, and linking the evaluation with the stakeholders' values, wishes, and future vision of the program, the use of Appreciative Inquiry ensures that the evaluation design and process will be as relevant and useful as possible (Preskill et al., 2003).

8. **Appreciative Inquiry complements systems thinking and complexity theory approaches.**

In today's rapidly changing and interdependent environments, programs frequently strive to develop, collect, and spread evidence and best practices about approaches that effectively address complex issues. Systems thinking and complexity theory are part of new paradigms in the field of evaluation that are helping it become more dynamic and useful in today's changing societal and organizational environments (e.g., see Westley, Zimmerman, & Patton, in press). The whole-systems nature of Appreciative Inquiry makes it complementary to systems thinking approaches in that it engages the "whole system" in the evaluation and encourages different parts of the system to talk to others; it helps participants understand everyone's contribution to the whole. It also enables all parts of a system to value the synergy created during exceptional performance moments of that system. Thus, participants and evaluators begin to explore the nature of their system in motion, appreciate human relationships and their organization's emotional capital, and identify best practices that help their organization perform at its peak.

AI is particularly effective in contexts and situations where the program design continues to evolve during the evaluation. In such cases, evaluation has a very important role to play in helping programs document their emerging models, record and validate their findings, evaluate their activities, and help identify and describe the evidence that needs to be shared across the organization. Under these circumstances, evaluation needs to be flexible and responsive to changing program realities. In this way, Appreciative Inquiry enables evaluation to evolve in response to the changing needs of organizations and programs.

## Summary

The very act of participating in an appreciatively oriented evaluation increases organization members' understanding of evaluation, and hopefully the value they place on evaluative inquiry. As organization members participate in the AI process, they begin to see how their stories and experiences relate to developing the program's logic model and the evaluation's design. They also see that the evaluation's purpose and key questions are not just haphazardly determined; rather, they are developed from what is learned from their stories. Furthermore, Appreciative Inquiry's use of paired interviews, from which themes of the participants' stories are identified, and the development of provocative propositions concretely connect evaluation to participants' real-life organizational issues and experiences. As a result, participants begin to understand how evaluation can support not only the organization's success but also their success as individual and team contributors.

Finally, Appreciative Inquiry supports organizational and evaluation capacity building by taking the fear out of evaluation (and inquiry in general), embracing a diversity of perspectives and experiences, building culturally competent and internationally relevant evaluation, exposing participants to reframing organizational challenges, clarifying linkages between programs and intended outcomes, and promoting learning, action, and change. Understanding its value, participants may be more likely to view evaluation as a worthy organizational function, and thus promote the use of results for learning and better decision making.

## Notes

1. This evaluation was conducted by EnCompass LLC, Potomac, MD, for *IREX (Education Review and Exchange Board)*. Reprinted with permission.

2. The evaluation was conducted by University Research Co. LLC, Potomac, MD. Reprinted with permission.

# Epilogue

## *Crossing Boundaries and Evaluation Innovation*

We started this book with the Prologue where we invited readers to consider integrating Appreciative Inquiry into their evaluation practice. Whether using AI in evaluation reflects a paradigm shift or merely one more tool for the evaluator's toolbox, we believe that it enriches the evaluation process and its findings and contributes to building organization members' evaluation capacity.

Perhaps the most challenging task for evaluators who want to use AI is learning how to reframe questions and issues to be appreciative. Gap analysis, problem solving, and deficit-based language are so ingrained in our discourse and cognitive processes that unlearning them is difficult. Even more demanding is to hold the course with client groups who continue to fall back to well-known and comfortable patterns of negativity. It is not unusual to find that after the paired interviews where stories, values, and wishes are shared, some people will follow up by saying, "The problem is. . . ." Evaluators must be prepared to help groups continuously reframe their dialogue and inquiry.

It is also important that evaluators be clear about their own comfort level with Appreciative Inquiry. There may be situations where the roles of the evaluator and the organization development practitioner merge and push the boundaries of either discipline. For example, the AI process may energize some clients to the point where they ask the evaluator to facilitate team-building activities, offer training on non-evaluation topics, provide coaching to managers concerning the implementation of certain evaluation findings, or lead other individual and organizational change activities. It is the evaluator's responsibility to make an honest assessment of his or her capability and interest, and the appropriateness of performing these tasks.

We believe that professions that learn from each other ultimately benefit organizations and society in general. While some may believe that drawing lines around an area of professional practice is desirable—that it helps to define and position the field—we think that moving these lines, or at least making these lines permeable, is beneficial. In this book, we have claimed that Appreciative Inquiry has much to offer evaluators and organizations. Yet incorporating AI into evaluation practice pushes the boundaries of traditional evaluation in ways that may not be met with approval by all professional evaluators. At the same time, Organization Development practitioners may wonder if adapting Appreciative Inquiry to evaluation where the entire AI process may not be used invalidates AI's purpose or impact. In spite of such concerns, we remain convinced that Appreciative Inquiry offers evaluators a meaningful and useful set of processes and tools that ultimately enhances evaluation practice and the quality of an evaluation's findings. As Webb, Preskill, and Coghlan (2005) write in their introduction to an issue of the *AI Practitioner* on evaluation and AI,

> There is great value that each field can bring to the other. Thus, we believe that a deeper understanding of and respect for the basic principles of each field is important in order to bring these two disciplines together. Individually, Appreciative Inquiry and evaluation have much to contribute to organizational effectiveness. Together, they can help organizations use creative and rigorous methods to build on the best of the past to create a desired future. The field of evaluation has begun to welcome Appreciative Inquiry for its power of reframing, and for its highly participatory processes. The field of AI is increasingly exploring the contributions of evaluation to organizational life, the tools and processes it offers for reflection and learning, and its commitment to utility by client and stakeholder groups of its findings, results, and processes. (p. 1)

Ultimately, we believe that such cross-fertilization stimulates creativity and innovation in both fields.

Incorporating Appreciative Inquiry into evaluation work can be exciting for evaluators who are passionate about enhancing learning from an evaluation, and who support the use of evaluation findings in ways that help create more hopeful and effective organizations. While Appreciative Inquiry is not the answer to all evaluations, it can make many evaluation studies stronger and better. The value of AI lies in its ability to offer evaluators another approach—one more way of contributing to organizational knowledge and success—to making evaluation ever more accessible and relevant.

# Appendix

## Using Appreciative Inquiry at Evergreen Cove

*Laverne Webb and Sherry Rockey*
*EnCompass LLC, Bethesda, MD*

When Sarah Sadler founded Psyche's Well in 1993, she envisioned a place where individuals could seek personal growth and development of mind, body, and spirit. A psychotherapist and long-time member of the human potential movement, Sadler brought her vision alive on the conservative, rural Eastern Shore of Maryland's Chesapeake Bay. The name was changed to Evergreen Cove Holistic Learning Center (EC) in 1999 with construction of a permanent facility nestled among old evergreens in a beautiful and peaceful cove on the Tred Avon River. The Center and its programs flourished, but its relationship to the larger community, especially the traditional health care system, did not. This sense of separation was reflected in the organization's view of itself, characterized by one practitioner as "fringe dwelling mystics."

Sadler and Evergreen Cove Board Chair Bradley Hower invited us to join them in thinking about an institutional development and long-term capital campaign program to support the growth and expansion of the programs and the membership base. They recognized that the worldview of holistic or alternative health was changing in significant ways. The language used in the healthcare arena foretold this change—alternative medicine was becoming known as complementary medicine, and even some insurance companies were beginning to reimburse services such as acupuncture. Our analysis suggested that EC might best begin with a focus on "friend raising" before it launched into a major capital campaign, and proposed using Appreciative Inquiry (AI) to accomplish this goal. As a result, EC launched the Appreciative Inquiry process in 2003 as Sadler was retiring and as Bob Hyman became the second generation of Evergreen Cove's leadership.

# The Appreciative Inquiry Process

### The Inquire Phase—Planning

Evergreen Cove enjoyed a special relationship with the practitioners who offered their services through the Center and sought to involve them in the AI process. They were invited to a visioning retreat with the board of directors, the new executive director, and EC staff to "begin a journey of conversations among ourselves . . . and then with the larger community, about the possibilities for our future . . . to answer the question, What is the world calling us to become?"

During this Appreciative Inquiry retreat, EC learned about the AI process, identified its core values, examined its factors of success, and identified its wishes for the future. The participants struggled with the dilemma of being open and listening to the larger community, and at the same time protecting the unique qualities of the Center that provide a safe space for the "fringe dwelling mystics" among them.

There were a few skeptics, and some had concerns about losing the close, supportive community they had created. Still, the group made a decision to go forward with the AI process and established a planning team. The planning team would guide the AI process over the next year, and the new executive director, in his debut appearance with the EC family, was charged to lead this work.

The planning team included four board and two staff members who launched its work several months after the retreat with the challenge of focusing the Appreciative Inquiry. To do this job well, the facilitator guided them in understanding and practicing the AI approach. Using AI interviews, they explored their vision, purpose, and expectations. They examined data from the appreciative interviews conducted at the retreat and engaged in a dialogue about what they had learned.

A key role of the planning team was to decide which stakeholders to include in the Appreciative Inquiry process. They settled on the following key groups: the EC community, donors, community groups, healthcare community, clergy, and retirees/newcomers. They also identified potential interviewers to be invited to an AI interview training session. The planning team was also charged with finalizing the AI questions. This team labored with getting the questions right, concluding that there were two audiences for this inquiry—the internal EC community, and the larger external community. In the end, the interview protocol reflected these differences.

### Training Interviewers

In this phase of AI, the facilitator conducted three half-day training sessions to prepare more than 50 interviewers. The goal of the workshops was to help people become ready to listen in a different way than they were used to. The interviewers were trained in the following interview techniques:

- Ensuring confidentiality

- Using a conversational tone

- Asking probing follow-up questions

- Keeping track of time without pressing the respondent

- Taking notes using the respondents' own words

- Reframing negative responses by helping the respondent to express what is desired rather than what is lacking

During the training sessions the participants had opportunities to experience the AI interview process and were given interview guidelines and tips for effective interviewing. The workshops also served the purpose of testing and refining the interview protocol and selecting stakeholders to contact for interviews. The planning team presented the trained interviewers with a list of stakeholders to be interviewed. During the training session each interviewer selected whom they preferred to interview from a stack of cards indicating the name and contact information for each potential interview. These cards were then used to track and manage the progress of the interview process.

## Conducting the Interviews

The interview team conducted over 125 face-to-face interviews lasting about one hour each between June and November 2003. Each interviewer was supplied with a packet of materials that included information about AI, effective interviewing tips, an introductory letter, an interview script, the interview protocol, a debriefing, and a sample thank-you note.

Each interviewer was asked to (a) send a letter of introduction to each individual on the contact list letting them know about the process and its objectives, and that the interviewer would be calling to schedule a meeting, (b) make a personal phone call to each individual to schedule a time for the AI interview, (c) follow the script and, using the AI protocol, conduct the interview, (d) ensure confidentiality, (e) use a friendly, conversational approach, (f) capture highlights of the story and positive ideas and images from the interview, (g) use the speakers' own words, (h) capture at least one great quote, (i) compile notes on the debriefing form provided in the packet and submit to EC either electronically or on paper, and (j) send a thank-you note to the interviewer. A sample of the AI questions shows the spirit and focus of the Inquiry:

### Topic I: Community

We live in many communities—families, neighborhoods, faith communities, where we work, our towns, for example. Today we want to explore what makes a community exceptional. Reflecting on your experience as a member of a community—one of these, or some other community—remember a high point, or an exceptional experience you had that enriched your life and/or that of the community. Tell me a story about that experience.

We see children and youth as important assets for the future of the community and the world. We hope to discover important ways Evergreen Cove could contribute to their support and development. Tell me a story that shows how the community, or an individual in the community, provided exceptional support for a child—either an experience you had, or one you have observed.

### Evergreen Cove Members or Program Participants Only

Many of our members have told us that they value the sense of community they experience at Evergreen Cove. They describe this community as a place where it is safe to be authentic, a nurturing place where one has a sense of connection, acceptance, and support, and a place where one can grow in mind, body, and spirit. Reflect back on your entire experience with Evergreen Cove and remember a time when you experienced this sense of safety, nurturance, support, or acceptance. Tell me a story about that experience.

### Topic II: Health

Good health is a treasure. It includes health of mind, and spirit, as well as body. If we have good health, many things are possible for us. Take a moment to think about what health means in your life. Tell me what health means to you. Tell me a story about a time you felt particularly healthy and alive.

Imagine that you live in a truly healthy community. What would be different from the way things are now? What steps could the community take to ensure a healthy future?

Values: What do you most value about yourself? This local community? Evergreen Cove?

Wishes: If you had three wishes for what Evergreen Cove might contribute to the health and vitality of our community over the next

5 to 10 years—something that would make the most difference to the future—what would they be?

## *The Appreciative Interview Data: Mining the Gold*

As the interviews were drawing to an end, EC began planning for the Evergreen Cove Summit on Healthy Communities. The facilitator convened a half-day "data mining session" for the planning team and a core group of interviewers to reflect on the interview process and the stories they had heard. The interview data had been entered into Excel spreadsheets and sorted by question and stakeholder groups. Stories and quotes that best illuminated each AI interview question were identified and later organized for use in the Summit conference. EC produced a "storybook" with illustrative stories and quotes for distribution along with invitations to the Summit participants.

This process created synergy as the group made meaning of the data. While focusing on the themes from the data, they had begun to collectively imagine what the organization would be like if such exceptional moments became the norm. This process inspired the planning team and interviewers for the *Imagine* Phase and the upcoming Summit conference.

## *The Imagine Phase*

The *Imagine* Phase asks the question, "What might be?" as interviewers and interviewees come together in a Summit conference to explore the positive past and create new images of the most desired and preferred future. During this Summit, Evergreen Cove, along with its key stakeholders in the community, answered the question, "What is the world calling us to become?" A macro vision for EC emerged out of this Summit that was used to focus the subsequent steps in the AI process.

## *The Evergreen Cove Summit on Healthy Communities*

This one-day Summit brought together over 50 participants—Evergreen Cove interviewers and a diverse cross section of the community members interviewed during the *Inquiry* Phase. Participants were invited to dream and imagine the possibilities for the future—to create shared images and visions for a healthier community.

The Summit conference began with an overview about Appreciative Inquiry and how EC was using this approach to reach out into the community and to plan its future. Participants then told stories from their most memorable AI interviews and explored themes that they saw emerging. To highlight the great diversity of stories, EC printed the exemplary stories identified in the "data mining" session onto cards that were placed at each table.

Participants read the stories on these cards and then shared them in small groups and in plenary, continuing to listen for common themes and patterns. Small groups examined the root causes of success in the stories and had a dialogue that led to clarifying the most enlivening, exciting possibilities for Evergreen Cove. Participants imagined ideal futures and created skits to bring them to life. Through an action planning exercise, they identified the most important activities Evergreen Cove should undertake to realize these visions. They then spoke to what they were individually ready, willing, and able to commit to help bring them into being.

There was a strong, resounding message that emerged from the common themes of the stories and from the visioning and planning exercises at the Summit—that Evergreen Cove has a valuable role to play by networking and bringing together players across the community in a dialogue about creating a healthy community. This message became the macro vision for Evergreen Cove that provided a focus for planning the next steps of the Appreciative Inquiry.

Evergreen Cove built on this foundation as it began planning to expand its Appreciative Inquiry work and engage a broader spectrum of the community, especially the health care system, in the next phase of AI—a community-wide forum on a healthy community to be conducted 3 months later.


## The Innovate Phase

In this phase of AI, organizations build on the visions and positive images of the future to create what is called "provocative propositions"—bold, actionable statements about that ideal future, written in present tense, as though they were already happening. These provocative propositions form the basis for creative and innovative strategies and actions for individual, organizational, and systems changes.


## Forum on Building a
## Vibrant Health Community

In the *Innovate* Phase of the AI process, Evergreen Cove sought to explore further the macro vision that emerged from the Summit. It began by recasting its annual Complementary and Alternative Health Expo to a "Forum on Building a Vibrant, Healthy Community"—advertised as a "Day for Mid-Shore Leaders and People Who Care About Our Future." Building on the foundation and vision articulated at the Summit conference, they set a goal:

"to establish a committed network of leaders and 'agents of change'—for knowledge sharing and learning—to discover, plan, and implement ways to move toward the future that we imagine and create together."

Evergreen Cove successfully enlisted new co-sponsors and Forum planners from every part of the health system, human service sector, education community, faith community, minority organizations, business community, and the arts. The planning committee assembled the most diverse group anyone could remember coming together in this community to participate in this phase of the Appreciative Inquiry process. Approximately 90 people attended the Forum.

The Forum began with a brief presentation on the research and theory of AI to set the stage for the paired appreciative interviews. The AI interview questions were designed to address the following topics:

- How do we each define health and well-being in our own lives?
- What does a vibrant, healthy community look like?
- How can we build on our positive past history and current strengths to promote a healthier community?
- What would an "epidemic of health and well-being" look like for our neighborhoods, organizations, and communities?
- How can we create this together?

The interviews began with participants sharing stories about a time when "you felt especially healthy and alive—or in a state of 'well-being.'" Participants told their interview partner's story in small groups, and many were then heard in plenary session. This process created a sense of understanding, shared values, and common ground. From these stories, small groups identified common themes and wishes and presented them to the plenary. In a large group dialogue, participants made meaning of these stories and themes through a guided discussion that explored what participants had heard, what inspired them, and what was most significant for the future.

The afternoon session focused on imagining the future together in small groups and creating visual artistic images that illustrated one or more themes from the stories. The "provocative propositions" were derived by an exercise that asked the small groups to imagine three years into the future when the *Washington Post* is writing a story on the "epidemic of health" on the Eastern Shore. The facilitator instructed the small groups to write this story, describing in some detail what is happening in this future time. Each group then presented its story and its visual image to the plenary group. These visions and stories formed the basis for working groups that would later become an ongoing initiative, the "Vibrant Community Initiative," implementing many of the ideas that grew from this one-day forum.

Several of the provocative propositions served to guide the work of the *Implement* Phase. A provocative proposition titled "Web of Interconnectedness" builds onto the overarching vision of EC that emerged from the Summit—EC as a convener of community dialogue about health and well-being. This provocative proposition reads,

> There is a vast connection of people and resources on the Eastern Shore. It appears that routine dialogue is occurring between those that have always lived here and those that have arrived recently. It is occurring in a myriad of ways, including watermen sharing their work with children, interdenominational youth activities, and mentoring programs involving older adults, children, and watermen. Barriers between institutions have fallen. The medical community has begun to recommend alternative/holistic therapies. Collaboration is occurring between individuals of varying economic, religious, and social groups. As a result, there are a plethora of activities available for all in the community.

The final exercise of the day was designed to deepen the understanding and commitment to appreciative processes. Participants were invited to write a five- to six-word personal vision statement tied to the key learning points they experienced through the AI process that day. By helping individuals see how an appreciative approach can affect change on a personal level, EC hoped to strengthen individual commitment to continue supporting the healthy community efforts.

## The Implement Phase

This phase is about grounding the visions, making the provocative propositions actionable, implementing change, and keeping the Appreciative Inquiry philosophy alive by creating an appreciative learning culture. It is during this phase that questions such as the following are addressed: "How can we make this happen?" "How do we navigate the change?" This phase introduces appreciative evaluation methods to keep groups oriented to their "true north." Appreciative evaluation promotes a culture of learning and knowledge sharing, as it takes the fear out of evaluation by promoting an appreciative learning leadership and culture.

## The Vibrant Community Initiative

Immediately following the Healthy Community Forum, Evergreen Cove hosted a meeting with the forum planning committee to review the themes, visions, and ideas for the future. This meeting served to generate support and commitment from planning committee members for the next steps. Shortly thereafter, they convened a larger group meeting with interested Forum participants. This group divided itself into task teams (e.g., healthcare, education, youth, elderly) that became known as the "Vibrant Community

Initiative." They also established meeting guidelines for each of these task teams that addressed not only organization and structure but also specified how they would continue to apply Appreciative Inquiry, including

- Use an appreciative approach: continue to focus on our community building vision; work from a place of abundance; build on the best from the past; share stories to create shared vision
- Appreciate successes: keep a list of team accomplishments; communicate successes to public; create a visual image of successes

The Vibrant Community Initiative task teams have continued their work. The task group on youth is planning an Appreciative Inquiry "Forum" event for young people. The Health Care task group is designing an AI approach to convening a "think tank" of health systems professionals and community and business leaders to explore alternative healthcare delivery models relevant to rural community needs. The task team on aging brought energy for new projects, including creating the *Seniors Resource Guide* and finding ways for seniors and youth to connect through volunteer activities—a vision created at the Healthy Community Forum.

In 2005, Evergreen Cove sponsored an annual reunion celebrating the Vibrant Community Initiative where task teams and other Healthy Community Forum participants came together to celebrate accomplishments and reinvigorate the spirit of the AI work. They used AI stories to dialogue about their past accomplishments and their hopes for the coming year, and they plan to keep the appreciative culture growing through a quarterly newsletter.

## Impact of the Appreciative Inquiry Process

Evergreen Cove made a significant commitment to the AI process as a way to engage its providers of holistic services and education programs with a diverse audience from the external community. The organization spent an entire year in conversations, listening to multiple voices and realities as they genuinely pursued the question, "What is the world calling us to become?" It was an act of courage and leadership for this "fringe dwelling" organization to reach out to the larger community. Many within the organization remained mindful of the risks of losing what made them unique. As EC pursued questions about health and well-being, about what an epidemic of health would look like, and about how they could support the community's visions, they too were changed.

The evolution of the organization is reflected in its new mission statement that refers specifically to community. The new statement reads: "To offer programs and services that nurture body, mind and spirit and cultivate community." The previous statement focused solely on the individual's health and well-being. Furthermore, EC's continuing commitment to growing an appreciative culture can be seen in its promotional materials that read, "Evergreen Cove—a community where the glass is more than half full, the days are mostly sunny, and there is plenty of room to grow." Without question, the vision and commitment of the executive director to both promoting and living the AI process plays a major role in the sustainability and institutionalization of AI in the organization and in the community.

### Evaluation of the EC Experience

In late 2004, EC conducted an evaluation of the EC project using the AI process. The purpose of the evaluation was to measure changes in perception, knowledge, and behavior among those who had participated in the AI process. The evaluation findings clearly demonstrate that the Appreciative Inquiry process had a significant and potentially long-term impact on Evergreen Cove. The Appreciative Inquiry process compelled EC to define and articulate its values and launched a dialogue within the organization and within the community that is helping EC clarify its visions for the future.

The act of engaging in an Appreciative Inquiry marked a distinct shift in how EC interacted with the community. Through the process of interviewing community leaders and members and inviting them to community discussions, EC generated a dialogue about health and well-being that put its philosophy and services at the center. Community leaders and health system leaders began to see EC in a new light. In fact, organization members have begun to see themselves in a new light.

By engaging the community, asking for its feedback, and responding with new programs and outreach, the AI process had a significant impact by focusing EC's agenda on community needs. People have begun to see EC as being connected to and concerned for the community. EC is now involved with sectors of the community and in activities that its members admit would not have happened before the AI process. The organization is working with the county health department, the school system, teens, seniors, and the under-served, as well as its core members.

One of the key objectives of AI was to increase growth of funding sources and revenue streams. In 2003, after the AI process began, EC increased its donor base by 50%. It has also been invited to form partnerships with mainstream health organizations and its increased visibility and reach in the community has laid the foundation for significant future increases of both individual and institutional supporters.

According to the evaluation findings, EC is now more recognized as a potential partner by the established health care community, and increasingly by the greater community. Becoming more visible has allowed some community members to see EC and its services as non-threatening and viable and as making an important contribution. However, the evaluation also indicated that widespread credibility and acceptance, especially in a conservative community, will take more time and concerted outreach efforts on the part of EC.

Finally, the evaluation highlighted some additional challenges that EC faces. Primary among them is the continuing debate among EC members about the organization's preferred image. While some longtime members of EC were concerned about becoming too mainstream, newer partners spoke of discomfort with EC as being on the fringes.

## AI Consultant Learning

The Evergreen Cove study provided a wonderful opportunity to experience and learn from an in-depth and full-scale Appreciative Inquiry. The techniques of AI are often applied to discrete activities or within limited time frames. A full-scale AI process requires a considerable commitment from the organization that is seeking change. Clearly, this level of commitment created significant change within Evergreen Cove. It also provided a wealth of learning opportunities for the consultants involved in the project.

Leadership and commitment are essential elements of success for an AI process. In a nonprofit organization this must include both the executive director and the board of directors or at least a majority of the board. Appreciative Inquiry presents a new worldview that requires leaders to develop appreciative leadership skills. AI is not a project or activity but rather a way of being in organizational life.

Taking time to plan properly is critical to a successful outcome. Planners become believers. The planning team must understand AI and be committed to it and to what it means to become an appreciative learning culture. This learning should be embedded throughout the AI process.

The diverse mix of individuals on a planning team ensures a deep understanding of the organization's systems, culture, priorities, and interests. A planning team that truly reflects the diversity of the organization is in the best position to address the questions that are most important for the organization's future.

Providing the right level and kind of support to the organization's leadership and planning team is important. The consultant often acts as a coach as well as a facilitator and must live and practice the AI philosophy in every way with the client. But it is important for the consultant to allow organization members to become champions of their own success and take ownership of the process and the results.

Engaging key stakeholders who do not seem to be fully supportive early and throughout the process can have longer term effects. In the Evergreen Cove case, resistant stakeholders were part of the decision about going forward in the initial retreat, and then invited to be part of the interviewer team, and/or were interviewed. By the end of the AI process, many resistant stakeholders came around to a very different relationship to the organization, and even became financial supporters.

The Evergreen Cove AI experience was a concrete reminder that AI processes do not, and should not, necessarily follow a strict formula. The processes need to be tailored to the organization and the context. The individual components of the process build on each other. They can also overlap and be used out of sequence. In this case, the steps from the *Inquire* Phase were used again in the *Innovate* Phase when the dialogue expanded to the broader community. In fact, the entire process was not planned from the beginning, but rather evolved from the circumstances and opportunities presented over time.

Helping the organization broaden the AI process and conversation to a broader community can help them reap the benefits from the AI process in the long run. When EC established an extended planning team for the Health Forum, the consultants took time to educate them about the AI process. In the Health Forum, we continued to teach about the AI philosophy and process as people experienced it and began to work together to imagine the preferred future. By the time EC had managed this second wave of an AI process, they had achieved ownership of the philosophy and approach and launched the Vibrant Community Initiative without any consulting assistance. They were teaching others and thereby teaching themselves at the same time.

# References

Abma, T. A. (2003). Learning by telling: Storytelling workshops as an organizational learning intervention. *Management Learning, 34*(20), 221–240.

Alkin, M. C. (Ed.). (2004). *Evaluation roots: Tracing theorists' views and influences.* Thousand Oaks, CA: Sage.

Alliance for Nonprofit Management. (n.d.). *Capacity building and organizational effectiveness.* Retrieved April 29, 2006, from http://www.allianceonline.org/about/capacity_building_and_1.page

Anderson, H., Gergen, K. J., McNamee, S., Cooperrider, D., Gergen, M., & Whitney, D. (2001). *The appreciative organization.* Taos, NM: Taos Institute Publications.

Ashford, G., & Patkar, S. (2001). *The positive path: Using appreciative inquiry in rural Indian communities.* Winnipeg, Canada: International Institute for Sustainable Development.

Banaga, G. (1998). A spiritual path to organizational renewal. In S. Hammond & C. Royal (Eds.), *Lessons from the field: Applying appreciative inquiry* (pp. 260–271). Plano, TX: Thin Book Publishing.

Barrett, F. J. (1995). Creating appreciative learning cultures. *Organizational Dynamics, 24*(2), 36–48.

Beecher, H. K. (1955). The powerful placebo. *Journal of the American Medical Association, 159*, 1602–1606.

Bens, I. (2000). *Facilitating with ease!* San Francisco: Jossey-Bass.

Berlew, D. E., & Hall, D. T. (1966). The socialization of managers: Effects of expectations on performance. *Administrative Science Quarterly*, p. 208.

Bradburn, N. M., Sudman, S., & Wansink, B. (2004). *Asking questions: The definitive guide to questionnaire design.* San Francisco: Jossey-Bass.

Bruner, J. (1971). *Toward a theory of instruction.* Cambridge, MA: Harvard University Press.

Bushe, G. (2000). Five theories of change embedded in appreciative inquiry. In D. L. Cooperrider, P. F. Sorensen, D. Whitney, & T. F. Yaeger (Eds.), *Appreciative inquiry: Rethinking human organization toward a positive theory of change* (pp. 99–109). Champaign, IL: Stipes Publishing LLC.

Cameron, K., & Caza, A. (2004). Contributions to the discipline of positive organizational scholarship. *American Behavioral Scientist, 47*(6), 731–739.

Cameron, K., Dutton, D., Quinn, R., & Spreitzer, G. *What is positive organizational scholarship?* Retrieved September 24, 2004, from http://www.bus.umich.edu/Positive/WhatisPOS/

Campbell, D. (2000). *The socially constructed organization*. London: H. Karnac Books Ltd.

Carpenter-Aeby, T., & Kurtz, P. D. (2000). The portfolio as a strengths-based intervention to empower chronically disruptive students in an alternative school. *Children in Schools, 22*(4), 217–231.

Catsambas, T., Kelley, E., Legros, S., Massoud, R., & Brouchet, B. (2002, December). The evaluation of quality assurance: Developing and testing practical methods for managers. *International Journal for Quality and Healthcare, 14*, Supplement 1, 75–81.

Catsambas, T., & Webb, L. (2000). *African Women's Media Center (AWMC) questionnaire analysis report*. Potomac, MD: EnCompass LLC.

Catsambas, T., & Webb, L. (2003). Using appreciative inquiry to guide an evaluation of the international women's media foundation Africa program. In H. Preskill & A. Coghlan (Eds.), *New Directions for Evaluation, 100*, 41–52. San Francisco: Jossey-Bass.

Cohen, B. Z. (1999). Intervention and supervision in strengths-based social work practice. *Families in Society, 80*(5), 460–466.

Connolly, P., & York, P. (2002). Evaluating capacity-building efforts for nonprofit organizations. *OD Practitioner, 34*(4), 33–39.

Cooperrider, D. L. (1999). Positive image, positive action: The affirmative basis of organizing. In S. Srivastva & D. L. Cooperrider (Eds.), *Appreciative management and leadership* (pp. 91–125). Euclid, OH: Williams Custom Publishing.

Cooperrider, D. L., & Whitney, D. (1999). *Appreciative inquiry*. San Francisco: Berrett-Koehler.

Cooperrider, D. L., & Whitney, D. (2000). A positive revolution in change: Appreciative inquiry. In D. L. Cooperrider, P. F. Sorenson, D. Whitney, & T. F. Yaeger (Eds.), *Appreciative inquiry: Rethinking human organization toward a positive theory of change* (pp. 3–28). Champaign, IL: Stipes Publishing.

Cooperrider, D. L., & Whitney, D. (2002). *Appreciative inquiry: A constructive approach to organization development and social change (a workshop)*. Taos, NM: Corporation for Positive Change.

Cooperrider, D. L., Whitney, D., & Stavros, J. M. (2003). *Appreciative inquiry handbook*. Bedford Heights, OH: Lakeshore Publishers.

Cousins, J. B. (1999). Organizational consequences of participatory evaluation. In K. A. Leithwood & K. S. Louis (Eds.). *Communities of learning and learning schools: New directions for school reform* (pp. 127–142). Amsterdam: Swets & Zeitlinger.

Cousins, J. B. (2003). Utilization effects of participatory evaluation. In T. Kellaghan & D. L. Stufflebeam (Eds.), *International handbook of educational evaluation* (pp. 245–266). Boston: Kluwer.

Cousins, J. B., & Earl, L., (Eds.). (1995). *Participatory evaluation in education*. Bristol, PA: Falmer Press.

Cousins, J. B., Goh, S., Clark, S., & Lee, L. (2004). Integrating evaluative inquiry into the organizational culture: A review and synthesis of the knowledge base. *Canadian Journal of Program Evaluation, 19*(2), 99–141.

Cousins, J. B., & Whitmore, E. (1998). Framing participatory evaluation. In E. Whitmore (Ed.), Understanding and practicing participatory evaluation. *New Directions for Evaluation, 80*, 5–23. San Francisco: Jossey-Bass.

Cronbach, L. J. (and Associates). (1980). *Toward reform of program evaluation.* San Francisco: Jossey-Bass.

Czaja, R., & Blair, J. (2005). *Designing surveys* (2nd ed.). Thousand Oaks, CA: Sage.

De Bono, E. (1985). *Six thinking hats: An essential approach to business management.* Boston: Little Brown & Co.

de Souza Silva, J. (2003, April). The basics of organisational capacity development. *Capacity.org, 17,* 3–4.

Dillman, D. A. (1999). *Mail and Internet surveys: The tailored design method.* New York: Wiley.

Dixon, N. (1994). *The organizational learning cycle: How we can learn collectively.* London: McGraw-Hill.

Edwards, J. E., Thomas, M. D., Rosenfeld, P., & Booth-Kewley, S. (1997). *How to conduct organizational surveys.* Thousand Oaks, CA: Sage.

Eitington, J. E. (2001). *The winning trainer* (3rd ed.). Houston, TX: Gulf Publishing.

Elliott, C. (1999). *Locating the energy for change: An introduction to appreciative inquiry.* Winnipeg, Canada: International Institute for Sustainable Development.

Fetterman, D. M. (2001). *Foundations of empowerment evaluation.* Thousand Oaks, CA: Sage.

Fetterman, D. M. (2005). *Empowerment evaluation principles in practice.* New York: Guilford.

Fink, A. (2003). *The survey kit* (2nd ed.). Thousand Oaks, CA: Sage.

Fitzpatrick, J., Sanders, J. R., & Worthen, B. R. (2003). *Program evaluation: Alternative approaches and practical guidelines* (3rd ed.). Boston: Allyn & Bacon.

Forss, K., Cracknell, B., & Samset, K. (1994). Can evaluation help an organization to learn? *Evaluation Review, 18*(5), 574–591.

Forss, K., Rebien, C. C., & Carlsson, J. (2002). Process use of evaluations: Types of use that precede lessons learned and feedback. *Evaluation, 8*(1), 29–45.

Fowler, F. J. (2002). *Survey research methods* (3rd ed.). Thousand Oaks, CA: Sage.

Franco, L. M., Newman, J., Murphy, G., & Mariani, E. (1997). *Achieving quality through problem solving and process improvement* (2nd ed.). Center for Human Services: Bethesda, MD.

Gibbs, D., Napp, D., Jolly, D., Westover, B., & Uhl, G. (2002). Increasing evaluation capacity within community-based HIV prevention programs. *Evaluation and Program Planning, 25,* 261–269.

Grayson, T. E. (2005, February). Discovering student learning outcomes and program strategies: An application of appreciative inquiry to evaluation. *AI Practitioner,* 12–15.

Groopman, J. (2004). *The anatomy of hope.* New York: Random House.

Haines, S. (2000). *The complete guide to systems thinking & learning.* Amherst, MA: HRD Press.

Hammond, S. A. (1996). *The thin book of appreciative inquiry.* Plano, TX: CSS Publishing.

Hammond, S. A., & Mayfield, A. B. (2004). *The thin book of naming elephants: How to surface undiscussables for greater organizational success.* Bend, OR: Thin Book Publishing Co.

Hardre, P. L. (2003). Beyond two decades of motivation: A review of the research and practice in instructional design and human performance technology. *Human Resource Development Review, 2*(1), 54–81.

Harrington-Mackin, D. (1994). *The team building tool kit.* New York: American Management Association.

House, E. R. (1993). *Professional evaluation: Social impact and political consequences.* Thousand Oaks, CA: Sage.

House, E. R. (2004). The role of the evaluator in a political world. *The Canadian Journal of Program Evaluation, 19*(2), 1–16.

House, E. R., & Howe, K. R. (1999). *Values in evaluation and social research.* Thousand Oaks, CA: Sage.

Huitt, W. (1997). Metacognition. *Educational Psychology Interactive.* Valdosta, GA: Valdosta State University. Retrieved October 9, 2004, from http://chiron .valdosta.edu/whuitt/col/cogsys/metacogn.html

Kelley, T., & Littman, J. (2001). *The art of innovations: Lessons in creativity from IDEO, America's leading design firm.* New York: Doubleday

Kretzmann, J. P., & McKnight, J. L. (1996). Assets-based community development. *National Civic Review, 85*(4), 23–30.

Krueger, R. A., & Casey, M.A. (2000). *Focus groups: A practical guide for applied research.* Thousand Oaks, CA: Sage.

Lave, J., & Wenger, E. (1991). *Situated learning: Legitimate peripheral participation.* Cambridge, UK: Cambridge University Press.

Levitan, S. A., & Wurzburg, G. (1979). *Evaluating federal social programs.* Kalamazoo, MI: The W. E. Upjohn Institute for Employment Research.

Liebler, C. J. (1997, Summer). Getting comfortable with appreciative inquiry: Questions and answers. *Global Social Innovations, Journal of the GEM Initiative, 1*(2), 30–40.

Livingston, J. A. (1997). *Metacognition: An overview.* Retrieved October 9, 2004, from http://www.gse.buffalo.edu/fas/shuell/cep564/Metacog.htm

Livingston, J. S. (1969). Pygmalion in management. *Harvard Business Review,* 16–31.

Ludema, J. D., Whitney, D., Mohr, B. J., & Griffin, T. J. (2003). *The appreciative inquiry summit: A practitioner's guide for leading large-group change.* San Francisco: Berrett-Koehler.

Ludema, J. D., Wilmot, T. B., & Srivastva, S. (1997). Organizational hope: Reaffirming the constructive task of social and organizational inquiry. *Human Relations, 50*(8), 1015–1052.

McLaughlin, J. A., & Jordan, G. B. (1999). Logic models: A tool for telling your program's performance story. *Evaluation and Program Planning, 22,* 65–72.

McLaughlin, M. W. (1975). *Evaluation and reform: The elementary and secondary education act of 1965.* Cambridge, MA: Ballinger.

McNamee, S. (2003). Appreciative evaluation within a conflicted educational context. In H. Preskill & A. Coghlan (Eds.), Using appreciative inquiry in evaluation. *New Directions for Evaluation, 100.* San Francisco: Jossey-Bass.

Meador, D. (1999). Measuring to report . . . or to learn? In P. Senge, A. Kleiner, C. Roberts, R. Ross, G. Roth, & B. Smith (Eds.), *The dance of change* (pp. 298–302). New York: Doubleday/Currency Publishing.

Mertens, D. M. (2005). *Research methods in education and psychology: Integrating diversity with quantitative and qualitative approaches.* Thousand Oaks, CA: Sage.

Merton, R. (1948). The self-fulfilling prophecy. *Antioch Review, 8,* 193–210.

Meyer, W. J. (1985). Summary, integration, and prospective. In J. B. Dusek (Ed.), *Teacher expectancies* (pp. 353–371). Hillsdale, NJ: Lawrence Erlbaum Associates Publishers.

Mohr, B. J., Smith, E., & Watkins, J. M. (2000). Appreciative inquiry and learning assessment. *OD Practitioner, 32*(1), 36–53.

Moore, C. M. (1994). *Group techniques for idea building.* Thousand Oaks, CA: Sage.

North Central Regional Education Laboratory. (n.d.). *Capacity building.* Retrieved April 29, 2006, from http://www.ncrel.org/sdrs/areas/issues/content/currclum/cu3lk24.htm

Norum, K. E., Wells, M., Hoadley, M. R., Geary, C. A., & Thompson, R. (2004). Ap-PRAISE-al: An appreciative approach to program evaluation. In D. L. Cooperrider & M. Avital (Eds.), *Constructive discourse and human organization: Advances in appreciative inquiry* (Vol. 1, pp. 193–214). London, UK: Elsevier Ltd.

Odell, M. (2002). *Beyond the box: An innovative Habitat for Humanity paradigm for participatory planning, monitoring and evaluation—measuring and increasing program impacts with appreciative inquiry.* Habitat for Humanity International.

Osher, D. (1996). Strengths-based foundations of hope. *Reaching Today's Youth, 1*(1), 26–29.

Owen, J. M., & Lambert, F. C. (1995). Roles for evaluation in learning organizations. *Evaluation, 1*(2), 259–273.

Owen, J. M., & Rogers, P. J. (1999). *Program evaluation: Forms and approaches* (2nd ed.). St. Leonards, Australia: Allen & Unwin.

Patton, M. Q. (1994). Developmental evaluation. *Evaluation Practice, 15*(3), 311–319.

Patton, M. Q. (1997). *Utilization-focused evaluation: The new century text* (3rd ed.). Thousand Oaks, CA: Sage.

Patton, M. Q. (2002). *Qualitative research and evaluation methods* (3rd ed.). Thousand Oaks, CA: Sage.

Posavac, E. J., & Carey, R. G. (2003). *Program evaluation: Methods and case studies.* Upper Saddle River, NJ: Prentice Hall.

Powell, D. S., & Batsche, C. J. (1997). A strength-based approach in support of multi-risk families: Principles and issues. *Topics in Early Childhood Special Education, 17*(1), 1–26.

Preskill, H. (2005). Evaluative inquiry. In S. Mathison (Ed.), *Encyclopedia of evaluation* (pp. 143–146). Thousand Oaks, CA: Sage.

Preskill, H., & Russ-Eft, D. (2005). *Building evaluation capacity: 72 activities for teaching and training.* Thousand Oaks, CA: Sage.

Preskill, H., & Torres, R. T. (1999). *Evaluative inquiry for learning in organizations.* Thousand Oaks, CA: Sage.

Preskill, H., Zuckerman, B., & Matthews, B. (2003). An exploratory study of process use: Findings and implications for future research. *American Journal of Evaluation, 24*(4), 423–442.

Redding, J. C., & Catalanello, R. F. (1994). *Strategic readiness: The making of the learning organization.* San Francisco: Jossey-Bass.

Roff, S. (2004). Nongovernmental organizations: The strengths perspective at work. *International Social Work, 47*(2), 202–212.

Rosenthal, R., & Jacobsen, L. (1968). *Pygmalion in the classroom: Teacher expectation and pupils' intellectual development.* New York: Appleton-Century-Crofts.

Rossi, P. H., Lipsey, M. W., & Freeman, H. E. (2004). *Evaluation: A systematic approach* (7th ed.). Thousand Oaks, CA: Sage.

Rossman, G. B., & Rallis, S. F. (2000). Critical inquiry and use as action. In V. J. Caracelli & H. Preskill (Eds.), The expanding scope of evaluation use. *New Directions for Evaluation, 88.* San Francisco: Jossey-Bass.

Roth, G. (1999). Cracking the "black box" of a learning initiative assessment. In P. Senge, A. Kleiner, C. Roberts, R. Ross, G. Roth, & B. Smith (Eds.), *The dance of change* (pp. 303–311). New York: Doubleday/Currency Publishing.

Rubin, H. J., & Rubin, I. S. (2005). *Qualitative interviewing: The art of hearing data* (2nd ed.). Thousand Oaks, CA: Sage.

Russ-Eft, D., & Preskill, H. (2001). *Evaluation in organizations: A systematic approach to enhancing learning, performance, and change.* Boston: Perseus Books.

Saleebey, D. (1992). *The strengths perspective in social work practice.* White Plains, NY: Longman.

Schwandt, D. R., & Marquardt, M. J. (2000). *Organizational learning: From world-class theories to global best practices.* Boca Raton, FL: St. Lucie Press.

Scriven, M. (1967). The methodology of evaluation. In R. W. Tyler, R. M. Gagne, & M. Scriven (Eds.), *Perspectives of curriculum evaluation* (pp. 39–83). Chicago: Rand-McNally.

Scriven, M. (1991). *Evaluation thesaurus* (4th ed.). Thousand Oaks, CA: Sage.

Senge, P. M. (1990). *The fifth discipline.* New York: Doubleday.

Stake, R. E. (2004). *Standards-based and responsive evaluation.* Thousand Oaks, CA: Sage.

Stevahn, L., King, J. A., Ghere, G., & Minnema, J. (2005). Establishing essential competencies for program evaluators. *American Journal of Evaluation, 26,* 49–51.

Stockdill, S. H., Baizerman, M., & Compton, D. W. (2002). Toward a definition of the ECB process: A conversation with the ECB literature. *New Directions for Evaluation, 93,* 7–26.

Talbot, M. (2000, January 9). The placebo prescription. *New York Times Magazine,* 34–39, 44, 58, 59–60.

Torres, R. T., Preskill, H., & Piontek, M. (2005). *Evaluation strategies for communicating and reporting* (2nd ed.). Thousand Oaks, CA: Sage.

van der Haar, D., & Hosking, D. M. (2004). Evaluating appreciative inquiry: A relational constructivist perspective. *Human Relations, 57*(8), 1017–1036.

Watkins, J. M., & Cooperrider, D. (2000). Appreciative inquiry: A transformative paradigm. *OD Practitioner: Journal of the Organization Development Network, 32*(1), 6–12.

Watkins, J. M., & Mohr, B. J. (2001). *Appreciative inquiry: Change at the speed of imagination.* San Francisco: Jossey-Bass.

Webb, L. D. (2000, May). AI in a public policy change process. *Appreciative Inquiry Newsletter, 9.*

Webb, L., Preskill, H., & Coghlan, A. (Eds.). (2005, February). Bridging two disciplines: Applying appreciative inquiry to evaluation practice. *AI Practitioner.*

Westley, F., Zimmerman, B., & Patton, M. Q. (in press). *Getting to maybe: How to change the world.* Random House Canada.

Whitney, D., & Trosten-Bloom, A. (2003). *The power of appreciative inquiry: A practical guide to positive change.* San Francisco: Berrett-Koehler.

Witherell, C., & Noddings, N. (Eds.). (1991). *Stories lives tell: Narrative and dialogue in education.* New York: Teacher's College.

Yelton, B., Plonski, P., & Edgerton, J. (2004, November). *Appreciative inquiry and evaluation: How's the fit? Spandex or flannel?* Round table session presented at the annual meeting of the American Evaluation Association, Atlanta, GA.

Zemke, R. (1999). Don't fix that. *Training Magazine, 36*(6), 26–33.

# Index

# About the Authors

**Hallie Preskill,** Ph.D., is a Professor in the School of Behavioral and Organizational Sciences at Claremont Graduate University. She teaches courses in program evaluation, Appreciative Inquiry, organizational learning, consulting, and human resource development. She coauthored *Evaluative Inquiry for Learning in Organizations* (Preskill & Torres, 1999), *Evaluation in Organizations: A Systematic Approach to Enhancing Learning, Performance & Change* (Russ-Eft & Preskill, 2001), *Evaluation Strategies for Communication and Reporting: Enhancing Learning in Organizations* (Torres, Preskill & Piontek, 2004), and *Building Evaluation Capacity: 72 Activities for Teaching and Training* (Preskill & Russ-Eft, 2004). Preskill also coedited "Using Appreciative Inquiry in Evaluation" (Preskill & Coghlan, *New Directions for Evaluation* #100, 2003) and the *Human Resource Development Review* (Russ-Eft, Preskill & Sleezer, 1997). Preskill has served on the Board of Directors of the American Evaluation Association (AEA) and the Academy of Human Resource Development, and will serve as the President of the AEA in 2007. She received the American Evaluation Association's Alva and Gunnar Myrdal Award for Outstanding Professional Practice in 2002 and the University of Illinois Distinguished Alumni Award in 2004. For over 20 years, she has provided workshops and consulting services in the areas of program evaluation, organizational learning, training design and delivery, and organization change, and has conducted program evaluations in schools, health care, nonprofit, human service, and corporate organizations.

**Tessie Tzavaras Catsambas,** M.P.P., is President of EnCompass LLC and brings 20 years of experience in evaluation, knowledge management, e-learning, and training. Ms. Catsambas is an innovator and practitioner in appreciative evaluation methods. Starting in 1998, she experimented with the use of Appreciative Inquiry in an evaluation of healthcare quality assurance activities in Chile. This became the first published work in appreciative evaluation in the *Journal for International Health Care Quality,* Volume 14, Supplement I, December 2002. She has continued to refine appreciative evaluation methods through her work with many clients in diverse settings including the World Bank, the United Nations, the Pubic Broadcasting Service, CARE International, the International Women's Media Foundation, and others. Ms. Catsambas brings her rich field experience to her training and has conducted annual training sessions at the American Evaluation Association Annual Conference since 2002. She has coauthored two chapters on appreciative evaluation methods (Preskill & Coghlan, *New Directions for Evaluation* #100, 2003). Her other clients include the U.S. Department of Labor, the Corporation for National and Community Service, the U.S. National Academies of Sciences, the U.S. Agency for International Development, Peace Corps, and the United Nations Foundation. She holds a Masters of Public Policy from Harvard University.